The Heath Workbook

Dusky Loebel
Tulane University

D. C. Heath and Company
Lexington, Massachusetts   Toronto

Contents

Chapter 8   # Writing Effective Sentences   63

Chapter 9   # Words   95

1

Understanding the Writing Process

1. Why Write?

For a moment, suppose that writing were not essential to communication in our culture but were instead an activity that we could choose to engage in or not. What benefits does writing offer as an activity pursued for its own sake?

a. Writing and perception

Writing heightens our awareness of the ways in which language shapes reality. Writing demands that we make deliberate choices from among many ways of identifying, hence perceiving, the features of our world. Consider, for example, the different implications of the following statements:

> Deborah is a loyal supporter of the president.
> Deborah is a devoted supporter of the president.
> Deborah is a zealous supporter of the president.
> Deborah is a fanatical supporter of the president.

Whenever we choose one label and reject another, we further define for ourselves the nature of the world.

b. Writing and thinking

By forcing us to give our ideas concrete form, writing also leads us to understand those ideas more fully. A written argument makes us attend to the quality and reasonableness of our ideas. Because it requires such precision, the act of writing is a powerful means of discovering and refining our ideas about any subject.

c. Writing and self-discovery

Writing not only leads to the discovery of new ideas, but also offers opportunities for discovery of the self. The commitment that is part of every important writing act forces us to consider what we really believe.

2. A Writer's Purpose

When we use writing to communicate our ideas to others, we place ourselves in a configuration of elements often referred to as the communication triangle:

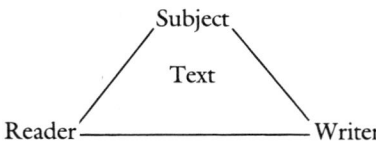

Because these interrelated elements vary endlessly, they demand great adaptability from writers. For example, when your readers change, so must your style and content. When your subject or your closeness to the subject changes, so must your tone. Finally, different kinds of writing, say, business letters and term papers, require you to follow different conventions.

Your "purpose" in writing means your awareness of the complex ways in which the components of each new communication triangle affect the content, style, tone, and form of what you write.

3. The Writing Process

Some people believe that writing should be a smooth act, word following word until all of their thoughts have been translated neatly onto the page. However, writing actually involves the far more complex process of discovering the meaning and implications of your ideas. Becoming aware of this process will make you a more competent and confident writer.

a. The recursiveness of writing

Most writers move forward only by repeatedly going back to an earlier point and rethinking what they have written. For that reason, writing can be described as a recursive process, one in which thinking, writing, and revising are not sequential steps but rather stages in a cycle that you repeat many times.

b. Avoiding frustration when you write

Writing is frustrating to everyone at one time or another. But you can reduce that frustration if you become more aware of your own writing process and the recursive quality of the act. Prepare for the fact that you probably will have to delete at least some of what you write, replacing it with ideas that will come to you only after you have immersed yourself in your writing.

In addition, pay attention to your own distinctive behavior as a writer. Becoming a good writer is partly a matter of identifying the habits that make you most productive and sticking to them whenever possible. Doing so may not make writing easy, but it will make it easier.

The form of this workbook requires that the different elements of writing and revising be presented in a linear order that is not true to the actual process of writing. Subject, audience, form, and purpose are interrelated, inseparable elements. Planning, writing, and revising are components of the process that constantly overlap.

Chapter 1

Exercise 1 The Writing Process

1. Write a short paragraph about the best writing experience you have ever had. It might have been the best because you were pleased with your product, because you enjoyed the process, or for any other reason.

2. Next, write a second short paragraph, describing your worst or least satisfying writing experience.

3. In a third, longer paragraph, fully analyze what accounted for the differences between the two. Consider deadlines, motivation, your topic, your audience, and so on. How might you apply your insights to future writing assignments? In what ways can you control whether writing will be a successful or an unpleasant experience for you?

2   *Discovering Ideas*

To be a successful writer, you need to know how to probe a subject for interesting angles to develop. Several strategies can make your thinking more productive. Keep in mind that the following methods won't be equally useful to every writer or in every writing situation. Experiment with several of the methods, and concentrate on the ones that seem to work best for you.

1. Unstructured Methods of Discovery

An unstructured method of discovery is one in which you let your mind go in whatever direction it chooses. The important task is to pay attention to this activity and make note of all the ideas it turns up. Only at the end of the discovery process, as you begin to shape your paper, should you go over your notes to decide which ideas you will use and which you will discard.

a. Brainstorming

Brainstorming is the free and uncontrolled play of the mind with an idea. The difference between brainstorming and mere random thought is that in a brainstorming session you write down all the ideas that come to you. The very act of noting each idea often prompts you to generate still more ideas. Do not edit them as you go, attempting to produce a neat, orderly list, because you might reject ideas that could be worthwhile later.

Many writers make a list as they brainstorm. Others like to use a mapping diagram. To do the latter, first write down on the center of the page the general topic. Then, as new ideas come to you, write them down on connecting lines drawn out from the center of the page, grouping related ideas together and extending the subgroups as far as possible. Like a list, the mapping diagram is also tentative and exploratory, and like any method of discovery, it will generate much more material than you will be able to use. Only when you have extended your ideas as far as possible should you go back to decide which ones might work in your paper.

b. Free writing

Free writing differs from brainstorming in that you attempt to catch the flow of your thoughts by writing them not as a list or a map but as a continuous thread of sentences. Free writing often begins with an idea or question that sparks your thought. Write the question down, and then follow it by quickly writing whatever comes to you. Don't attempt to focus, pause, or edit; your object is to maintain the rapid flow of thought and to fill your pages with writing, not to compose a coherent essay on the spot.

c. Keeping a journal

Journal writing differs from free writing in several ways. Whereas free writing is a rapid, almost unconscious activity, writing in a journal is a more reflective one. In addition, a journal presumes a kind of continuity; you collect entries so that you can go back to reconsider what you have written. A journal is probing and speculative rather than merely factual. It is also personal, not because its contents are private but because the journal reflects your own outlook on the world.

Journal writing calls for discipline. Although there is no "right" or "wrong" way to keep a journal, you do need to write in it regularly, perhaps daily. Remember that journal writing, like other unstructured methods of discovery, may raise questions that you have no conclusive answers for but that lead you to additional ideas.

2. Structured Methods of Discovery

Structured approaches to discovery follow an orderly plan, usually a fixed set of questions to answer or a checklist of topics to consider.

Journalistic questions

Most people are familiar with these questions: Who? What? When? Where? Why? How? By expanding this formula with additional questions under each of these main headings, we can create a useful structured-discovery approach.

WHO?	Who is involved in X?
	Who benefits from X?
	Who suffers because of X?
WHAT?	How is X defined?
	How would you describe X?
	What is X similar to?
	What parts make up X? How are they related to one another?

WHEN?	When did X occur?
	How long did X last?
	What events preceded X?
	What events followed X?
WHERE?	In what setting did X occur?
	What other circumstances made X possible?
	How might X have been different had the circumstances been different?
WHY?	What are the causes of X?
	What are the consequences of X?
HOW?	How did X come to be?
	Who made X?
	How does X work?

Your goal is not to provide a single answer to each question but, rather, to try to produce as many responses as you can. Also, recognize that not every question will be relevant to every topic. As with brainstorming and free writing, your initial task is to collect as much diverse information about your subject as possible. Later, as you begin to organize your paper, you will be able to choose the best ideas and consider how they can be most effectively organized and developed.

Exploring a subject in this systematic way takes concentration, persistence, and imagination. It can also help to make you a writer with something worth saying.

Chapter 2

Exercise 1 Brainstorming

Using the brainstorming technique of either listing or mapping, explore one of the general topics below. Generate as many ideas as you can in one sitting; wait a few hours and then return to the subject. Repeat this procedure several times, and then review all the ideas you have discovered. Which ideas do you think you could turn into an interesting essay?

1. Owning a pet
2. Helicopters
3. Cartoons
4. Gardening
5. Dentists
6. Fires

Chapter 2

Exercise 2 Free Writing

Using free writing, write steadily for ten minutes on one of the following topics. At the end of ten minutes, select what you consider to be the most important or interesting idea in your free writing. Copy that idea onto the top of a clean page, and write again for ten minutes. When you have finished, underline the best ideas from your two sessions and rewrite them into a single coherent paragraph.

1. Your fondest memory from your childhood
2. What you most regret having said to someone
3. One historical event you wish you could have witnessed
4. What you would most like to be able to change about your family
5. That sport which seems most valuable to American culture

Chapter 2

Exercise 3 Structured-Discovery Questions

In Exercise 1 you used brainstorming to explore a subject. Now examine the same subject using the expanded set of journalistic questions listed in Section 2 of the introduction to this chapter. Remember, you may find that some of the questions are not relevant to your topic, but consider each one carefully before you decide.

Chapter 2

Exercise 4 Comparing Discovery Methods

In Exercise 2 you used free writing and in Exercise 3 you used a set of questions to explore the same topic. Carefully review your responses to both exercises. Which approach to discovery—unstructured or structured—produced the most useful or interesting responses? Write a paragraph explaining why one method or the other works best for you.

3   *Considering Your Audience*

The term *rhetoric* has long been associated with the concept of persuasion. However, *rhetoric* may also refer more broadly to the use of language in order to produce any effect in an audience of readers or hearers. Virtually every act of human communication contains a rhetorical element. At the very least, we want the people around us to believe that we are worth listening to. Inspiring that belief in our audience is itself a rhetorical act.

1. The Rhetorical Situation

The relationship between you and your audience is called the **rhetorical situation.** When writing, you can only imagine how readers will react to what you write. To be a good writer, you must be able to alter your writing to suit widely different audiences and rhetorical situations.

2. Analyzing Audiences

Unfortunately, there is no such thing as the "general reader." Once you recognize that your audience is never people in general but always a particular selection of people, you need to consider ways of identifying and understanding those persons, for only then can you write effectively for them. The following list of questions can help you with this task.

Questions for analyzing audiences

Audience's background

What do I know about my audience's
age?
social status?
level of education?
political positions?
moral beliefs?

Audience's relation to subject and writer

What does my audience already know about this subject?
What else do I want my audience to know?

What do I want this audience to think of me as a person?
What evidence or arguments will be convincing to this audience?

Not all of these questions will be relevant in every case. But for most writing tasks, this checklist will provide a helpful way of reflecting systematically on your audience and rhetorical situation.

Chapter 3

Exercise 1 Considering Your Audience

Choose a problem at your university that you think could be remedied. Write two letters explaining why this problem needs attention and how it might be solved. Your audience in one letter is the dean or president of the school; your audience in the other is the student newspaper. Begin by applying the questions for analyzing audiences to both. Be prepared to discuss how your awareness of audience affected the content, organization, and tone of both letters.

1. Analysis of first audience:

Letter 1:

2. Analysis of second audience:

Letter 2:

4   *Choosing a Voice*

Writing begins as dialogue. As a writer you do not have to give up the sense of self that enlivens conversation; you can create in your writing many of the different voices you use in speaking.

1. A Writer's Voice

Your written voice, like your speaking voice, can vary in tone from ironic to passionate, from annoyed to outraged, from humorous to grim. The first step in developing your voice is recognizing that you can make choices. To a large extent, the voice in your writing—also called the tone—depends on your attitude toward your subject and your reader.

2. Voice and Subject

Before you can write with any distinguishable voice, you must decide how you feel about your subject. You need not (and probably will not want to) explicitly express that attitude. Instead, to convey your attitude you must rely on carefully chosen words and details. Even apparently objective writing results from a decision—your decision *not* to reveal your attitude toward the subject.

3. Voice and Audience

Equally important to your tone is the relationship that you seek to establish with your readers, one that changes with each rhetorical situation you face.

a. Great distance between writer and reader

Certain types of writing, such as scientific or other kinds of informative writing, sometimes (but not always) call for great distance between you and your reader. You can create this distance by using a highly technical vocabulary, avoiding personal pronouns and contractions, and writing in passive voice. Such formal writing implies that your main interest is your subject rather than your reader.

b. Moderate distance between writer and reader

Informative writing need not be impersonal. To create moderate distance between you and your reader, you can use relatively formal diction but occasionally include a personal pronoun or a contraction.

c. Moderate intimacy between writer and reader

Using the personal pronouns *I* and *you* can help you to draw the reader into your writing, creating an informal or even intimate tone.

d. Great intimacy between writer and reader

To create an even closer bond with your audience, you can use personal pronouns, contractions, colloquial diction, and slang. Such a tone, of course, is usually inappropriate for college assignments.

No absolute rules can help you to determine how to approach your readers. Instead, you must think carefully about the kind of relationship with them that is appropriate to each particular rhetorical situation.

Chapter 4

Exercise 1 Voice and Subject

Write three paragraphs on one of the following topics. The *content* of the three should be similar, but the voice should be different in each. Make your voice in the first paragraph as neutral as possible. In the second, create a voice that reflects a positive attitude toward your subject. In the third, express through voice a negative attitude toward your subject. Finally, analyze the specific differences among the three paragraphs.

1. Your first week at college this semester
2. Some aspect of a job you have had
3. A pet
4. Your roommate or a neighbor

Paragraph 1:

Paragraph 2:

Paragraph 3:

Analysis:

Chapter 4

Exercise 2 Voice and Audience

Choose from Exercise 1 one of the topics that you did not use. Write two paragraphs about this new topic. In the first, create a voice that reflects great distance between you and your reader. In the second, create a voice that reflects intimacy between you and your reader. Then analyze the specific differences between the paragraphs.

Paragraph 1:

Paragraph 2:

Analysis:

Chapter

5 *Organizing an Essay*

1. Limiting Your Subject

To write effectively, you need to be able to limit the scope of a subject. College writing in all disciplines provides you with practice in deciding what is important about your subject. Although there are no easy procedures for limiting a subject, recognizing the role of purpose and audience in this process can lead you to ask some useful questions as you approach any writing task.

a. Consider what you know about yourself

What aspect of your subject is most interesting or important to you? Why? Use your background and inclinations to steer yourself toward subjects that you will be able to write about with genuine interest.

b. Consider what you know about your readers

If you could tell your readers only one thing about your subject, what would it be? Why? You can narrow a paper on any topic by regarding it as an essay with a specific point that you want your readers to carry away with them.

2. Formulating a Thesis Statement

As your understanding of your precise subject evolves, try to formulate your controlling idea in a single sentence or two: a **thesis statement.**

a. Components of a thesis statement

A thesis statement often begins as a tentative expression of the main point of your paper. In its final form, however, your thesis must be specific and unambiguous, for it establishes your readers' expectations about what is to follow. A thesis usually contains two elements: the precise subject of the essay, and a word or two that further restricts the subject.

Subject	Possible restricting phrases
	threatens the existence of many cities in the American West.
The pollution of underground water supplies	is difficult to detect.
	has reached serious proportions in the American West only within the past twenty years.

A clear thesis often implies a method of development. The first thesis above will lead to an exploration, the second will be more technical in nature, and the third might offer a historical perspective.

b. Precision in a thesis statement

Make sure your thesis contains the actual topic you intend to develop, not just a generalized topic.

Vague	Many experiences help a person develop respect for the rights of others.
Precise	Sharing a college dorm suite with five other students helps a person develop respect for the rights of others.

Sometimes the problem with a thesis is not that its stated subject is too vague but that the thesis does not limit the subject adequately.

Vague restriction	The Vietnam War had a great effect on this country.
Precise restriction	The Vietnam War years created divisions in American society that have lasted into the 1990s.

A thesis statement should not merely announce what you intend to do in a paper.

Announcement with no restriction	In the following paper, I will discuss my decision to spend my senior year as an exchange student in Ireland.

Precise subject and restriction

I decided to spend my senior year in high school as an exchange student in Ireland because I wanted to learn about my family's ancestors.

Avoid thesis statements that rely on formulas, such as "This paper will examine. . . ."

c. Placement of a thesis statement

Very often you will want to place your thesis statement near the beginning of your essay, often in the opening paragraph. Placed there, it provides for the reader a way of focusing attention, giving him or her a head start in comprehending the ideas that follow. In addition, such a thesis statement constantly reminds you, the writer, of the direction your paper should be taking. Theoretically, you may place a thesis statement elsewhere in the essay, as long as it is prominent enough for the reader to recognize it as your thesis.

3. Organizing Ideas

Sometimes the subject itself of a paper will determine the best arrangement of your ideas, such as occurs when you are writing a paper that describes a process or narrates an event. Many topics, however, do not suggest a clear structure. Begin by formulating as precise a thesis as you can, and then experiment with several ways of arranging your supporting ideas, each based on a different approach. You will need to consciously search for a pattern.

4. Writing an Introduction

In general, your introductory paragraph should attract and hold the reader's attention, should indicate the subject matter of the paper, and should reveal in some way your attitude toward the subject. You can usually write an effective introduction only *after* you have formulated your thesis statement. You might even consider writing your introduction after you have written the rest of the paper.

a. Beginning with the thesis statement

One way of getting started is to begin with your thesis. Later on, you can go back and discard or revise your introduction.

b. Beginning with a quotation

Occasionally, you might begin your introduction with a quotation that closely ties in with your thesis. If your subject is a published work, you might open with a quotation from that text.

c. Building up to the thesis statement

The most sophisticated introduction is one that gradually builds up to your thesis, enabling you to begin with background information that establishes a context for your main point. A thesis in this position also leads smoothly into the first paragraph of the body of your paper.

No matter what form of introduction you use, confidence, authority, and solid content characterize the most successful opening paragraphs.

5. Shaping the Body of an Essay

As you think about how to present your ideas in the body of your paper, plan to develop points that are approximately equal in importance with equal amounts of evidence and discussion. Devote more space to any ideas that you wish to emphasize.

You can achieve appropriate emphasis through arrangement as well as balance. Consider beginning with the least important facts, examples, or arguments and moving to the most important. If you use your best evidence first, the rest of your paper may seem anticlimactic.

6. Writing a Conclusion

A very short essay may not require a conclusion. More often, though, you will need one. Your conclusion should consist of more than a sentence or paragraph attached to the end of an essay with a transition like "Therefore . . ." or "In conclusion. . . ."

a. Ending with a sense of finality

The best conclusions mark the arrival of the essay at the destination announced in its introductory paragraph, thereby giving your reader a sense of finality.

b. Ending by echoing the introduction

Often you can create a feeling of completion by recalling a word or phrase from your introduction. However, avoid mechanically restating your introduction.

c. Ending by bringing ideas together

Particularly in a long or complex paper, you might conclude by drawing connections among ideas you have explored in the paper.

7. Constructing Outlines

a. Uses of outlines

Perhaps the most important use of the formal outline is to help you organize ideas generated during the discovery stage of the writing process. The more complex the topic and the more elaborate its supporting evidence, the more essential outlining becomes.

Outlines also assist you when you revise a rough draft or an unsatisfactory final version of your paper. When a paper seems to lack coherence, balance, or tight logical structure, a formal outline of its contents can help you diagnose the problem.

Finally, outlines often provide a useful way of examining the plan and structure of another writer's work.

b. Types of outlines

The **paragraph outline** is a list of sentences numbered so that sentence 1 summarizes paragraph 1, sentence 2 summarizes paragraph 2, and so on. This type of outline helps you review the progression of major ideas in a paper and is often a good starting point in planning an essay.

The **topic outline** begins with the entire thesis statement. After that, its entries are words or brief phrases, numbered and lettered to show the relative importance of the paper's supporting ideas.

Each entry in a **sentence outline** is a complete sentence. For long papers, this type of outline may be the most useful because it enables you to consider thoroughly the contents of the paper.

c. Conventions of topic and sentence outlines

The following system of alternating numbers and letters is nearly universal in outlines.

Thesis
I.
    A.
        1.
        2.
            a.
            b.
    B.
        1.
        2.
II.
    A.
    B.
    C.

Use Roman numerals to indicate the major subdivisions of the idea stated in your thesis. Mark further subdivisions with capital letters, Arabic numbers, and small letters. Indent coordinate points—those of equal importance—the same distance from the left margin; under them, farther in, place subordinate or supporting points. Remember that each subdivision must consist of at least two entries; in other words, an outline may not have an "A" section without a "B" section or a "1" section without a "2" section.

Chapter 5

Exercise 1 Restricting a Thesis Statement

Complete each of the following potential thesis statements in two different ways by adding two different restricting phrases.

1. Having many brothers and sisters . . .

2. A house in the country . . .

3. Not allowing children to watch television . . .

4. Time spent alone . . .

5. Learning to play the drums . . .

Chapter 5

Exercise 2 Recognizing and Restricting a Thesis Statement

Explain why each of the following statements is *not* a workable thesis statement as it stands. Rewrite each in two different ways, restricting the topic.

1. Houseplants are available in many varieties.

2. This paper will examine why I chose to attend college.

3. A good diet is an important part of staying healthy.

4. Growing old is an experience we all must face.

5. Gun control remains a controversial subject.

Chapter 5

Exercise 3 Outlines and Introductions

1. Using one of the thesis statements you wrote for Exercise 1 or 2 (or a topic your teacher assigns), write a detailed outline of a possible essay on the topic.

2. Next, write two different introductions for the same essay. Which introduction do you like better? Why?

Chapter 5

Exercise 4 Conclusions

Using the same topic for which you wrote an outline and two introductions in Exercise 4, write a possible conclusion. In what ways does the conclusion do more than just repeat in different words your introduction?

6   *Constructing*
Paragraphs

1. Recognizing Paragraphs

Paragraphs have a primarily *rhetorical* function: they help your reader identify and follow your main ideas. Underlying this rhetorical concept of a paragraph are two principles. First, a paragraph should ordinarily be unified around a single topic. Second, if your reader is to make sense of the text, all the paragraphs in a piece of writing must be related to one another in some ascertainable way. As a writer, be prepared to discover paragraphs in your writing where you had not previously seen them. Look for opportunities to combine short paragraphs, be ready to divide long ones, and don't hesitate to move a sentence from one paragraph to another.

2. Using Topic Sentences

Sometimes you will succinctly state the main idea of a paragraph in a sentence known as a **topic sentence.** Just as a thesis statement directs the reader's attention to the central idea in an essay, a topic sentence, when it exists, helps the reader more readily grasp your point. Like a thesis, a topic sentence usually introduces both a subject and a specific focus. And like a thesis, a topic sentence is in some sense an arguable statement, one that leads to, or even demands, specific support or proof in the rest of the paragraph.

a. Formulating a topic sentence

Consider these two sentences:

> Abraham Lincoln was born in what is now Larue County, Kentucky.

> As more and more good cooks are discovering, a food processor is an indispensable kitchen tool.

Because it does not raise an idea that needs further comment but instead simply states a fact, the first sentence could not be a strong topic sentence. The sentence presents a clear subject, but it does not present a focusing idea. In contrast, the second sentence has both a clear subject, *food processor,* and a controlling focus, *indispensable*. Such a sentence prepares the reader for the direction the paragraph is going to take.

Organizing paragraphs around topic sentences in your first draft can help you generate content for each paragraph by focusing your attention on the specific point you must develop. Keeping your topic sentences in mind as you revise an essay is a way of checking that all sentences in a paragraph really belong there.

b. Positioning a topic sentence

Placed near the beginning of a paragraph, a topic sentence arouses your reader's expectations about the paragraph's development. However, you may place a topic sentence anywhere—after a transitional sentence, in the middle of a paragraph, or at the end as a kind of conclusion. When a topic sentence comes in the middle of a paragraph, it usually links the sentences that precede it with the material that follows it. When a topic sentence concludes a paragraph, it usually pulls together sentences that have led up to it. In these cases, the subject and focus of the paragraph are left implied until the reader reaches the topic sentence.

The practice of constructing a paragraph around a topic sentence is useful, but a paragraph may be unified even though it does not contain an explicit topic sentence. The important thing is that your main idea be evident to your reader. An implied topic sentence works only when the development of the paragraph leaves no room for doubt about its point. Most of the time, you should make an effort to include a topic sentence somewhere in the paragraph, rather than risk leaving your reader uncertain about your main idea.

3. Adjusting Paragraph Length

Just as the structure of a paragraph is designed for the reader's benefit, so is the length of a paragraph determined by its helpfulness to the reader. The key question is always this: how much evidence is required to develop the idea in the topic sentence?

Ordinarily, a paragraph should be longer than one sentence but shorter than a page. However, the length of paragraphs varies considerably in different kinds of writing. If you are in doubt about the length of a paragraph you are working on, ask yourself the questions about structure discussed above:

What is the main idea in this paragraph?
Have I provided enough evidence, detail, or discussion to develop it to my reader's satisfaction?

Have I included irrelevant material that should be moved to another paragraph or discarded?

a. Using a short paragraph for emphasis

Occasionally, you may want to use a very short paragraph to draw attention to an important shift in your argument or to emphasize a key point. Such paragraphs are effective, but use them carefully and sparingly.

b. Paragraphing dialogue

In a narrative, any direct quotation, together with the rest of the sentence of which it is a part, is paragraphed separately:

"But 'glory' doesn't mean a nice 'knock-down argument,' " Alice objected.

"When *I* use a word," Humpty Dumpty said in a rather scornful tone, "it means what I choose it to mean—neither more nor less."

However, you may include in one paragraph brief dialogue that is closely related to the narration.

My wife looked at me with irritation. She was heading toward a boil. Then she looked at the blind man and said, "Robert, do you have a TV?"

Chapter 6

Exercise 1 Recognizing Topic Sentences

Identify the subject and specific focus, if any, of each of the following statements. Which of the statements could make good topic sentences? Briefly explain why.

1. Foreign imports are the best cars on the market in this decade.

2. The early years of Paul McCartney's career were his most creative.

3. Sharing an apartment with a roommate is not always a wise idea.

4. Many new college students do not know what major they want to pursue.

5. The development of atomic weapons profoundly and permanently altered the entire concept of warfare.

6. Chocolate is almost everyone's favorite flavor.

7. The first thing to consider when you are choosing a new doctor is convenience.

8. Obtaining a pilot's license is a challenge.

9. When I left the house yesterday morning, I had no idea that my life would change so quickly and dramatically.

10. Not every person requires eight hours' sleep a night.

Chapter 6

Exercise 2 Positioning Topic Sentences

Choose one of the following topics. Write three similar paragraphs on it, narrowing the topic as necessary. Place the topic sentence in a different position in each. Which version do you think is most effective? Explain your answer.

1. Why _____ is the best actor performing in the movies today

2. The main reason to attend college

3. Why I prefer the brand of _____ that I buy

4. America's most important environmental problem

Chapter 6

Exercise 3 Analyzing Topic Sentences

Examine the last essay you wrote. For each paragraph, answer the following questions.

1. What is the topic sentence, if any, in the paragraph?
2. How effective is the topic sentence?
3. Could the topic sentence be more effectively positioned elsewhere in the paragraph?
4. If the paragraph lacks a topic sentence, does it need one? (If so, supply such a sentence here.)

Paragraph 1

1.

2.

3.

4.

Paragraph 2
1.

2.

3.

4.

Paragraph 3
1.

2.

3.

4.

Continue this analysis for each paragraph in your essay.

7 *Developing Paragraphs*

What happens in a paragraph—the form that its contents assume—is often determined by the subject itself. In a narrative, for example, chronological order will probably dictate the structure of your material. Sometimes, however, your subject may not arrange itself with inevitable clarity and logic. For these occasions, you need to be acquainted with a number of basic patterns of paragraph development. Controlling these patterns is another way of making your writing more effective by satisfying your reader's expectations. Keep in mind that in actual practice, you will rarely use these strategies independently of one another but instead will find that they naturally overlap. Regard these patterns less as a set of alternatives than as a master list of techniques to select from and combine freely.

In addition, consider these approaches as ways of not simply arranging the contents of a paragraph but also generating content for both paragraphs and entire essays. Phrased as questions, they can help you find new angles of your subject to write about.

1. Development by Specific Detail

Part of your task as a writer is to supply the details necessary to support the main idea of a paragraph. To write with specific detail, begin by recalling as precisely as possible the event you are to describe and then recreate it with carefully chosen words. Often you can dramatically improve a paragraph by simply substituting specific details for generalities. Make sure that those details are relevant to your purpose; select them carefully. Details become boring—mere padding—if you confuse quantity with quality.

2. Development by Narration

Effective narration, reporting what happened and in what sequence, depends on your exact selection of details, arranged in such a way that your reader can easily follow the order of the events. Sometimes a paragraph of narration includes a topic sentence that focuses its development on a specific idea. But a narrative paragraph doesn't always need a thematic focus, or even a topic sentence, to hold it together; chronology alone may be sufficient.

3. Development by Examples

An example is a member of a larger class or category, chosen to illustrate the class to which it belongs. Typically, the topic sentence of a paragraph developed by examples introduces the general class. For instance, your topic sentence might state the class "contaminants in the workplace," and in the rest of the paragraph you could discuss cigarette smoke, photocopiers, and computer screens. Often examples are introduced with the transition *for instance* or *for example*. Even without these markers, the structure of the paragraph will be evident to your reader if you clearly state at the outset the categories the examples illustrate.

4. Development by Definition

Definition involves referring a term to a general class of related elements (its genus), and then distinguishing it from others in that class.

Term	*Class*	*Differentiation*
pen	writing instrument	makes use of a hard point and colored fluid
pencil	writing instrument	has a core of solid material like graphite inside a wooden or plastic case

When you are writing about complex terms or about terms used in a special sense, you may need to devote a paragraph or more to definition. Make sure that you avoid circular definition, a faulty approach that uses the term being defined in the definition itself. Also, avoid definition composed of long lists of synonyms—precision is more important than sheer volume. Finally, avoid loaded definitions, ones that rely on inflammatory language ("Euthanasia is the outright murder of a helpless human being"); their purpose is usually emotional manipulation rather than clarity.

5. Development by Classification

When you use classification to develop a paragraph, you enumerate and describe the main divisions of a subject, either for clarification or as an introduction to further discussion. Underlying classification is the notion that the elements of any large group—classic cars, home computers—can be divided into a number of subgroups and that classification will better help the reader to understand the category as a whole.

A classification makes sense only if you group the things being classified according to some clearly understood principle or feature. The second characteristic of a successful classification is that it is exhaustive; all the members of the larger group must fit into one or another of the categories.

6. Development by Comparison or Contrast

When you wish to point out the similarities or differences between two subjects, comparison or contrast is the natural method of development. Comparisons are usually structured in one of two ways. In the first, **alternating comparison,** you switch back and forth between two subjects throughout the paragraph, creating for the reader a point-by-point comparison. In the second type, **divided comparison,** you fully discuss the first subject before turning to the second, thereby dividing the paragraph approximately in half. This latter approach works well when the subjects cannot be compared point by point and you are more interested in developing each at length.

7. Development by Analogy

An analogy is a comparison between two essentially unlike things, one familiar to the reader, the other less familiar. A clever analogy can sometimes make a difficult concept easier to understand. Make sure that you regard the analogy as an illustration, though, not as proof.

8. Development by Cause and Effect

In the cause-and-effect method of development, the emphasis is on the connections between a result or results and the preceding events. A cause-and-effect paragraph may begin by stating an effect and then explaining its causes, or it may open with a cause and go on to explore its effects. More often, however, causes and effects are intermingled in a subtler way.

Although all of these methods of development are useful at times for developing entire paragraphs, normally you will use a combination of them, especially in longer paragraphs.

Chapter 7

Exercise 1 Developing Paragraphs by Specific Detail

Write two different paragraphs on one of the following topics. In the first paragraph, make the diction as vague and general as you can. In your second paragraph on the same subject, substitute specific detail to make your description vivid and interesting.

1. Sounds at the beach
2. Your first impressions of your dorm room or some other spot on campus
3. A main street in your hometown
4. The atmosphere of your least favorite restaurant
5. A student studying at the last minute before an exam

Chapter 7

Exercise 2 *Developing Paragraphs by Narration*

Write a paragraph developed by narration on one of the following topics. Begin by listing points you might include and, if possible, formulating a topic sentence.

1. The first time you drove a car
2. Buying textbooks at college for the first time
3. The last time you visited an eccentric relative
4. The way you usually get ready for a date
5. Your first stay in the hospital

Chapter 7

Exercise 3 Developing Paragraphs by Examples

Write a paragraph developed by examples on one of the following topics. Begin by listing points you might include and, if possible, formulating a topic sentence.

1. The importance of studying another language
2. The disadvantages of owning a car
3. Ways to stay in good physical condition
4. The influence of space travel on the American public
5. The benefits of urban renewal

Chapter 7

Exercise 4 Developing Paragraphs by Definition

Write a paragraph developed by definition on one of the following topics. Begin by listing points you might include and, if possible, formulating a topic sentence.

1. Charm
2. Junk food
3. Common sense
4. A good cup of coffee
5. The ideal football stadium

Chapter 7

Exercise 5 Developing Paragraphs by Classification

Write a paragraph developed by classification on one of the following topics. Begin by listing points you might include and, if possible, formulating a topic sentence. Try to find a method of classification that is not obvious or predictable.

1. Insects
2. Public television programs
3. Blue jeans
4. Movie-theater seats
5. Detective fiction

Chapter 7

Exercise 6 Developing Paragraphs by Comparison or Contrast

Write a paragraph developed by comparison or contrast on one of the following topics. Begin by listing points you might include and, if possible, formulating a topic sentence.

1. Halloween when you were a child and now
2. Two houses or apartments you have lived in
3. The Marx Brothers and the Three Stooges
4. Waterskiing and downhill skiing
5. Fraternities and sororities

Chapter 7

Exercise 7 Developing Paragraphs by Cause and Effect

Choose two of the following topics, one from the causes category and one from the effects category, and write two separate paragraphs. Begin by listing points you might include and, if possible, formulating a topic sentence.

Analyze causes

1. Choosing not to vote in national elections

2. Attending a particular movie: _____

3. Participating in a particular sport: _____

4. Choosing to play a certain musical instrument: _____

Analyze effects

1. Living in a small town
2. Having a new baby in the house
3. Witnessing an automobile accident
4. Dropping out of college

Chapter 7

Exercise 8 Developing Paragraphs by Another Method

Choose one of the topics that you wrote about in the other exercises in this chapter. Write a paragraph on the same topic developed by a different method. For example, if you defined *charm,* now try contrasting it with a slightly different concept, such as *charisma*. Pick a subject that interests you. As you write, pay attention to the way in which the choice of a method of development may affect how you think about a subject.

8 *Writing Effective Sentences*

Although the precise source of a writer's style is difficult to isolate, the study of sentence style does repay your effort. Through it, you can appreciate more fully the mastery of other writers and also enlarge your own repertoire of stylistic skills. If concentrating on your sentence style—unity, conciseness, rhythm, emphasis, and smoothness—is a new experience for you, you at first may find it difficult to break old habits. But stylistic skill will come with practice.

1. Writing Unified Sentences

A unified sentence makes its points clearly, and all of the details in it have a clear relationship to one another and to the main idea of the sentence. Two major problems may interefere with sentence unity.

a. Too many ideas

The first way to create unity in a sentence that rambles from point to point is to identify the separate ideas in it. Then group them in order to divide the sentence into two (or more) different ones.

Problem sentence	Many people objected when the cry for women's suffrage was first heard, and the opposition continued for decades, until finally opponents began to realize that women were entitled to the vote, and in 1920 the Nineteenth Amendment was ratified.
Sentence 1	Many people objected when the cry for women's suffrage was first heard.
Sentence 1	The opposition continued for decades.

Sentence 2	Finally opponents began to realize that women were entitled to the vote.
Sentence 2	In 1920 the Nineteenth Amendment was ratified.
Revised as two sentences	Many people objected when the cry for women's suffrage was first heard, and the opposition continued for decades. Finally, however, opponents began to realize that women were entitled to the vote, and in 1920 the Nineteenth Amendment was ratified.

A second way you can create unity is to eliminate unimportant ideas. List the distinct ideas in the sentence and reconsider their importance to its main point.

Problem sentence	Inexpensive word processors, which first became available to the public in the late 1970s and which, like other technological innovations such as computer chips and digital recording, are part of what sociologists call the postindustrial revolution, have made a significant dent in the electric typewriter market, which includes secretaries, students, and teachers, among others.
Keep	Inexpensive word processors first became available to the public in the late 1970s.
Eliminate	Inexpensive word processors, like other technological innovations such as computer chips and digital recording, are part of what sociologists call the postindustrial revolution.
Keep	Inexpensive word processors have made a significant dent in the electric typewriter market.

Eliminate	The electric typewriter market includes secretaries, students, and teachers, among others.
New sentence	Inexpensive word processors have made a significant dent in the electric typewriter market since they first became available to the public in the late 1970s.

Neither of these two strategies alone may help you unify some disorganized sentences. You may need to divide the sentence *and* to scrutinize its contents for extraneous ideas.

b. Faulty coordination and subordination

Coordinate constructions define two or more sentence elements as equally important. Most coordinate constructions are formed with coordinating conjunctions: *and, but, for, or, nor, yet,* and *so.*

Subordinate constructions, on the other hand, define elements in a sentence as unequal in importance, thereby focusing the reader's attention on the more important one. Subordinating words fall into two categories:

Relative pronouns

that	whichever	whomever
what	who	whose
whatever	whoever	
which	whom	

Subordinating conjunctions

after	before	than	where
although	even though	though	whereas
as	how	unless	wherever
as if	if	until	whether
as though	since	when	while
because	so that	whenever	

Sometimes you can use either a coordinate or a subordinate construction to separate ideas into a single unified sentence, depending on whether you wish the reader to perceive the ideas as equal or unequal in importance.

Ideas to be combined	Matthew checked the spelling in the report. Theresa checked the calculations.

| Coordinate construction—equal importance | Matthew checked the spelling in the report, and Theresa checked the calculations. |
| Subordinate construction—unequal importance | While Matthew checked the spelling in the report, Theresa checked the calculations. |

The clause that follows the coordinating conjunction is called the subordinate clause; the other clause, on which the emphasis of the sentence falls, becomes the main clause.

Sentence unity collapses when you use a coordinating conjunction to connect ideas that are unrelated or unequal in importance:

| Lacks unity | Elizabeth Michaels chaired yesterday's meeting and is the company's newest computer expert |

Place one of these elements in a subordinate clause, depending on the emphasis you want to give each.

| Unified | Elizabeth Michaels, who chaired yesterday's meeting, is the company's newest computer expert. |
| Unified | Elizabeth Michaels, who is the company's newest computer expert, chaired yesterday's meeting. |

Sentence unity also collapses when you place the main idea of a sentence in a subordinate construction and thereby draw your reader's attention to the less important idea.

| Lacks unity | As Mr. Stevens drove off the road, he tried to kill a bee inside the car. |
| Unified | As Mr. Stevens tried to kill a bee inside the car, he drove off the road. |

2. Writing Concise Sentences

Superfluous words weaken a sentence. The difficulty is knowing what to strike out and what to retain in order to include all the essential information without wasting words.

a. Redundant words, phrases, and clauses

Redundancy is a flood of words that repeat the same ideas.

The criticisms I want to make are major ones *that you ought to consider carefully because of their importance.*

Common redundant phrases to watch for include the following:

attractive in appearance	cooperate together
repeat again	young in age
several in number	

b. Nominalizations

The noun form of a verb is called a **nominalization.** Nominalizations may weaken your writing if you use them instead of more direct verbs.

Wordy	It is the city council's *intention to make a decision about* the future of Maple Street Park at tomorrow's meeting.
Concise	The city council *intends to decide* the future of Maple Street Park at tomorrow's meeting.

Such writing occasionally is called the bureaucratic style. Below is a list of common nominalizations and their more direct equivalents.

Nominalization	*More concise verb*
I am of the belief that	I believe
She reached the conclusion that	She concluded
We held a discussion of	We discussed
We are in need of	We need
I will conduct a study of	I will study
They made a recommendation of	They recommended

c. Wordy connectives

Join elements in your sentences as directly and economically as possible.

Wordy	Sarah is studying German *because of the fact that* she hopes to become an interpreter.

| Concise | Sarah is studying German *because* she hopes to become an interpreter. |

Here are some wordy connectives and their more concise equivalents.

at this point in time	now
due to the fact that	because
during the period when	when or while
in order to	to
in the event that	if
the majority of	most
on the occasion when	when

d. Unnecessary repetition

Eliminate repetition that creates awkwardness rather than emphasis. Try reading your writing out loud to catch such repetition.

| Wordy | The problem of the homeless is *a formidable problem*. |

| Concise | The problem of the homeless is *formidable*. |

e. Overuse of the passive voice

A verb is in the active voice when the grammatical subject of the sentence performs the action presented in its predicate: *She wrote* the book.

Occasionally, the thing or person acted upon is more important than the one who acts. In this case, the sentence can be written in the passive voice, with the object or recipient of the action placed in the subject position: Her *book was nominated* for the Pulitzer Prize.

A passive verb is both appropriate and necessary when the one who acts in the sentence is not known: My *car* apparently *was stolen* during the night. In most writing, however, the actor is more important than the recipient of the action. In addition, passive verbs are always less concise than active ones.

| Wordy passive | After my first draft has been completed and the paper has been set aside for a day or two, revising is begun by me. |

Concise active	After I have completed my first draft and have set the paper aside for a day or two, I begin revising.

Passive constructions often obscure the true actor in a sentence.

Passive	The changes that had been made in the conservation bill by the committee were accepted by the Senate, which voted to pass the bill.
Active	The Senate passed the conservation bill that the committee had amended.

f. *There is* and *it is* constructions

The common constructions *there is* and *it is*—called **expletives**—are in many cases acceptable sentence openers:

There is no reason to doubt her honesty.

It is true that he had been drinking before the accident.

But used carelessly, these constructions add words that contribute nothing to the meaning of the sentence.

Wordy	It was in 1927 that Virginia Woolf published her novel *To the Lighthouse*.
Concise	Virginia Woolf published her novel *To the Lighthouse* in 1927.

3. Creating Parallelism

In writing, the ordering of like element with like element is called **parallelism**, or **parallel structure**. Parallel structure balances word with word, phrase with phrase, subordinate clause with subordinate clause.

Parallel words and phrases

It is often the failure
who is the pioneer in

new lands,
new undertakings,
and new forms of expression.

—Eric Hoffer

Parallel clauses

The *Iliad* is only great because all life is a battle,
the *Odyssey* because all life is a journey,
and the book of Job because all life is a riddle.

—G. K. Chesterton

Parallel sentences

Children begin by loving their parents.
After a time they judge them.
Rarely, if ever, do they forgive them.

—Oscar Wilde

Parallelism is indispensable for good writing. Below are some guidelines for creating parallel sentences.

a. Coordinate pairs

All sentence elements joined by *and, or, nor, for,* and *but* should be in like grammatical structures.

Faulty	He likes *reading* all the books he can lay his hands on and *to write* whenever the mood strikes him.
Parallel	He likes *to read* all the books he can lay his hands on and *to write* whenever the mood strikes him.
Parallel	He likes *reading* all the books he can lay his hands on and *writing* whenever the mood strikes him.
Faulty	Students in composition classes learn *to read* with attention and *that* coherent essays must be written.

Parallel	Students in composition classes learn *to read* with attention and *to write* coherent essays.
Parallel	Students in composition classes learn *to read attentively* and *to write coherently*.

b. Elements in a series

Three or more elements in a series must be grammatically parallel to one another.

Faulty	I concluded that she was *intelligent, witty,* and *liked to make* people feel at home.
Parallel	I concluded that she was *intelligent, witty,* and *hospitable*.

c. Repetition of words

Sometimes you will need to repeat a conjunction, preposition, or other preceding word to make a construction parallel.

Unclear	The vineyard is often visited by tourists who sample *grapes* and *connoisseurs* of wine.
Clearer	The vineyard is often visited *by tourists* who sample grapes and *by connoisseurs* of wine.

d. Correlatives

Conjunctions that occur in pairs are called **correlatives**: *either . . . or, neither . . . nor, not only . . . but also, both . . . and*. The parts of speech immediately following each conjunction must be identical.

Faulty	William Blake is *not only famous for* his poetry *but also for* his illustrations.

Parallel	William Blake is famous *not only for* his poetry *but also for* his illustrations.
Faulty	He *either is* a liar *or* a remarkably naive person.
Parallel	He *either is* a liar *or is* a remarkably naive person.
Parallel	He is *either a* liar *or a* remarkably naive person.

e. Subordinate clauses

A subordinate clause is never parallel to the main clause in a sentence. Do not connect it to the main clause by *and* or *but*.

Faulty	She is a woman of strong convictions and who says what she thinks.
Correct	She is a woman of strong convictions who says what she thinks.
Parallel	She is a woman *who has* strong convictions *and who says* what she thinks.

f. Sequence of ideas

Make elements that are parallel in grammatical structure parallel in sense. Used carelessly, a parallel construction can lead to an illogical series or an awkward sequence of ideas.

Illogical	Her many friends, her recent marriage, and her slumping business could not offer Amy the happiness she had known while she was in college.
Correct	Neither her many friends nor her recent marriage could offer Amy the happiness she had known while she was in college.

4. Writing Cumulative and Periodic Sentences

A cumulative sentence states its main idea first and then follows it with modifying words, phrases, or clauses. Such a sentence is clear, direct, and relatively easy to control.

> *I began to keep a journal* when I discovered that my life was interesting, my dreams colorful, and my thoughts surprisingly profound.

In a periodic sentence, the main idea is held until the end; the sentence begins with all the subordinate details. A periodic sentence can effectively engage your reader, who is made to continue reading until you reveal your point.

> When I discovered that my life was interesting, my dreams colorful, and my thoughts surprisingly profound, *I began to keep a journal*.

Placed strategically after several cumulative sentences, the periodic sentence has an emphatic effect. To use a periodic sentence effectively, however, make sure that the main idea is important enough to receive such emphasis.

5. Varying Sentence Length

When all the sentences in a passage are approximately the same in length and structure, the results can make for tedious reading. To avoid monotonous prose, simply vary the length and structure of your sentences.

6. Varying Sentence Openers

When every sentence in a passage begins with its subject, the effect is also tedious. Experiment with alternate openings.

a. Single modifiers

> The exhausted street musician began to pack up his equipment.
>
> *Exhausted*, the street musician began to pack up his equipment.

b. Prepositional phrases

The weather in this city is completely unpredictable.

In this city, the weather is completely unpredictable.

c. Inversions

In an inverted sentence, the normal word order (subject-verb-complement) is reversed by placing the complement before the verb. Use this construction sparingly.

Judy's red hair was barely visible behind the piles of paper on her desk.

Barely visible behind the piles of paper on her desk was Judy's red hair.

d. Appositives

Although usually placed after the nouns they refer to, appositives can precede them and may begin a sentence.

Those stained-glass windows, a gift of the college's first graduate, are irreplaceable.

A gift of the college's first graduate, those stained-glass windows are irreplaceable.

e. Verbal phrases

Look for opportunities to convert verbs in a sentence into participial or gerund phrases as beginning elements.

Al was worried about the legal implications of the document and refused to sign it.

Worried about the legal implications of the document, Al refused to sign it.

f. Absolute phrases

An absolute phrase, usually made up of a noun plus an adjective or participle, is a distinctive sentence opener.

Jill's patience was exhausted, and she began to raise her voice.

Her patience exhausted, Jill began to raise her voice.

g. Adverbial clauses

Moving an adverbial clause to the beginning of a sentence adds emphasis and changes a cumulative sentence into a periodic one.

The mayor refused to sign the proclamation, because most of the city council members advised against it.

Because most of the city council members advised against it, the mayor refused to sign the proclamation.

Chapter 8

Exercise 1 Unity

Improve the unity of the following sentences by dividing them into separate sentences, by eliminating unnecessary information, and/or by using the appropriate coordinate or subordinate constructions.

1. Hansen's disease is more commonly known as leprosy and to this day has horrible connotations and the disease is widely misunderstood.

2. It is an ancient disease, while references to leprosy in the Bible, for example, are deceptive, since the term was used for many kinds of disfiguring ailments, not just what we now know as Hansen's disease, or leprosy.

3. In those biblical times and ever since, the disease has been thought to be extremely contagious, and in fact it is not.

4. Because the spouses of afflicted people and the professionals who care for them are very rarely infected, infection seems to require prolonged contact and special circumstances.

5. The disease is named after Armauer Gerhard Hansen, a man who was a Norwegian doctor who discovered sometime in 1879 the microorganism that causes it.

6. Much research has been done since that time, and the public remains misinformed about the symptoms of Hansen's disease, which often are not as extreme as people think.

7. While in most cases the results are skin discoloration and minor skin lesions or nerve damage, only in rare cases does mutilation result, and most often because a loss of sensation in the extremities may lead to accidents.

8. Unfortunately, in the past the false beliefs about Hansen's disease and the social stigma of being a "leper"—a word no longer used because of the connotations—led to victims being ostracized, and they were isolated in leprosariums, and some of these are still in existence today, such as the one that is in Carville, Louisiana.

9. Now sulfone drugs are used to arrest the development of the disease, and reconstructive surgery often repairs any disfiguration, and rehabilitation often helps the patient lead a normal life.

Chapter 8

Exercise 2 Unity

Improve the unity of the following sentences by dividing them into separate sentences, by eliminating unnecessary information, and/or by using the appropriate coordinate or subordinate constructions.

1. Someday you may find you need an excuse to take a holiday, and you don't have to wait until the Fourth of July or New Year's Eve.

2. While almost every day of the year marks an anniversary or birthday or has been specially designated by someone somewhere, some of these holidays are religious, and they retain the original sense of the word, which was "holy day."

3. Many religious holidays have been secularized, and they have taken on a more popular than sacred meaning, since Groundhog Day began as a religious celebration and was called Candlemas.

4. You might not care to remember Valentine's Day, which is on February 14, and you could instead celebrate some other occasion, such as the birthday of Copernicus, Oregon Statehood Day, and, in Liberia, Literacy Day.

5. In March, you might choose to observe the anniversary of the Girl Scouts on the twelfth, which is when the organization was founded, or, if you are really desperate, the anniversary of the Milwaukee Public School Music Festival on the twenty-sixth of March.

6. April offers several birthdays to celebrate, including those of Bette Davis, who was an actress, and Ulysses S. Grant, and April 10 is Salvation Army Founder's Day, although April 15 is the federal income tax deadline.

7. August 26 is the anniversary of the Nineteenth Amendment, and in 1920 it granted voting rights to American women.

8. You need not limit yourself to American holidays, since if you are interested in Scandinavia you could celebrate the anniversary of the Norwegian constitution on May 18 or, in Denmark, Constitution Day, which is on June 6.

9. Greeting-card companies and florists have profited from such holidays as Secretary's Day and Grandparents' Day, and they might want to look into a list such as this one, and then they could broaden their market even more.

Chapter 8

Exercise 3 Concise Sentences

Revise the following sentences to make them more concise.

1. Although people in the modern world in which we live in the late twentieth century may scoff at superstitions, many people still continue to cross their fingers for luck, carry good-luck charms, avoid cats that are black in color, and feel uneasy breaking a chain letter sent to them.

2. The majority of superstitions, for the most part, seem to have no grounding in reality.

3. For example, the view of thirteen as an unlucky number originally started long ago in ancient times and seems to be a foolish belief.

4. Nonetheless, the construction of many buildings built in the mid-twentieth century is such that they have no thirteenth floor.

5. On the other hand, however, some old superstitions actually have a real, factual basis.

6. Garlic frequently appears in many superstitions as a remedy for various ailments and as a protector to guard against evil spirits.

7. Doctors at this current period in time are considering now whether garlic may indeed actually have beneficial effects.

8. Similarly, the Western medical establishment of doctors and scientists is also reevaluating and reconsidering the healing properties of herbs, which other cultures have long respected in their societies.

9. Many people are of the belief that the full moon brings out strange and odd behavior.

10. Is that just yet another superstition, or will it one day in the future be substantiated by science?

11. When contemplating various and different cultures or even our own, twentieth-century skeptics might remember to keep in mind that the line between superstition and science may not always be as clear as it seems to appear.

Chapter 8

Exercise 4 Concise Sentences

Revise the following sentences to make them more concise.

1. In the event that your only exposure to golf has been to tournaments broadcast on television, you have seen the best in the world but missed experiencing the fun of playing the real sport.

2. The game of golf is an outdoor game offering moderate exercise, neither too strenuous nor too easy.

3. If you make a decision to learn the game of golf, you should probably take lessons.

4. Since the fundamentals are so important to your enjoyment of the game, proceed to make contact with a player who will spend four to six hours of his or her time teaching them to you.

5. After you learn the basics and fundamentals, the probability exists that your game will improve only with practice.

6. No matter what your skill level is that you have reached, you will probably make the discovery that the most enjoyment consequently results from playing with friends of about the same ability you have attained.

7. Because of the fact that personalities may change on a golf course, avoid playing with a friend who is much better or more accomplished than you.

8. You do not always have to plan ahead every time when you want to play golf.

9. If you are in need of partners, go to the first tee at a course and pick up a game.

10. Just remember, never gamble or play for money with strangers whom you do not know.

Chapter 8

Exercise 5 Passive Voice; It is/there are Constructions

Eliminate ineffective passive voice and *it is* or *there are* constructions in the following sentences.

1. It is claimed by mailings and television announcers every day, "A million dollars could be won by you!"

2. Often, there is no understanding by winners that a large percentage of the value of a prize must be paid to the U.S. government in taxes.

3. Cars, for example, often must be sold in order for the tax to be paid, which can be as much as 30 percent of the price of the vehicle.

4. It is true that some lucky people win contests that did not have to be entered, such as when a winning license plate is chosen at random.

5. There are few such prizes that are unclaimed, however, even when the company does not notify the winner, because the details are often published in national newletters.

6. A lot of energy is devoted by a surprising number of people to following these contests, and newsletters are read faithfully.

7. Occasionally, letters are mailed to uninformed winners by unscrupulous readers of these newsletters, and the offer is made for information about the prize to be given in exchange for a large "finder's fee," sometimes as much as several thousand dollars.

8. Fortunately, it is often that winners are notified by readers who are generous and write or call simply out of kindness and curiosity that is felt.

9. With all the contests that are being held, there are very many people who could be the next winner—but caution should be taken by them.

Chapter 8

Exercise 6 Parallelism

Revise the following sentences to correct faulty parallelism.

1. I am a bird lover and who likes to have bird feeders in my backyard.

2. Unfortunately, I fight a continuing battle with squirrels to keep them away from the feeders and not letting them eat all of the bird food.

3. Squirrels are very aggressive, and such preventive measures as mounting feeders on greased poles or hung from wires will not stop these creatures, which are both clever and they persist in their attempts.

4. Although homemade feeders are not only useful because they are inexpensive but also they are rewarding to make, they are particularly susceptible to squirrels.

5. One day in my backyard, a cob of corn hung from a chain disappeared, both cob and the chain.

6. Next I tried a plastic feeder, which I made from an empty one-liter soda bottle by drilling a hole through it, inserting a stick in the hole for a perch, and which had another hole to allow the birds to reach the seed with their beaks.

7. This bottle, hung from a bush with a thin, foot-long wire and to be filled with sunflower seeds, baffled the squirrels temporarily.

8. However, because squirrels have sharp teeth and that they are resourceful, they gnawed through the plastic, enlarged the feeding hole, and they reached the food.

9. After that, they went so far as to make the hole even larger so that they could lie in the feeder and eat until they had all they wanted or emptying the feeder.

10. Now I have given up, and I buy sunflower-seed holders that either are made of metal or of heavy plastic.

11. The squirrels are still able to climb down, to get the seeds, and interfere with the birds, but at least they are slowed down and that they can't de-stroy the feeders.

Chapter 8

Exercise 7 Parallelism

Revise the following sentences to correct faulty parallelism.

1. Although some residents of coastal areas may have "hurricane parties" or refusing to evacuate, people who have survived a hurricane know that it is nothing to celebrate, to welcome, or take lightly.

2. The power of a hurricane is suggested in the name itself, which comes from roots that both mean "storm god" and "evil spirit."

3. Because hurricanes can be more than five hundred miles in diameter and that they have winds well over two hundred miles per hour, most coastal dwellers understand their danger and prepare for them.

4. Often hurricanes are accompanied by tornadoes, rain, and also by storm tides.

5. The worst hurricane in U.S. history hit Galveston in 1900, to level the island and killing six thousand people.

6. In 1969, Camille took the lives of more than three hundred people and severely damaging property in the Southeast.

7. Naming hurricanes, after either women as was first done or, now, after women and men, may be a way of trying to view an uncontrollable force as something more human, more tamable, and as being less terrifying than it really is.

8. However, all people can do is to prepare for an approaching hurricane and controlling their own response to it.

Chapter 8

Exercise 8 Cumulative and Periodic Sentences

By adding different sets of appropriate modifiers, rewrite each of the following sentences, first as a cumulative sentence and then as a periodic sentence. Decide which version you prefer and why.

1. The Salem witch trials of 1692 are an infamous and misunderstood episode in American history.

2. Many people are unaware that the number of so-called witches executed was twenty.

3. Many people also do not realize that none of the victims was burned at the stake.

4. In New England the condemned were hanged or, in one instance, pressed to death.

5. The panic began when two girls began behaving strangely and accused various people of bewitching them.

6. Modern psychologists might attribute the panic to mass hysteria on the part of the accusers and the accused.

7. Other scholars have pointed to the role of social pressure in the trials.

8. Some of the accused were simply eccentrics who refused to conform to strict standards of decorum.

9. The topic has been exploited by makers of television movies.

10. Students of history need to understand what really happened in Salem.

Chapter 8

Exercise 9   Varying Sentence Openers

All of the following sentences begin with the subject. Rewrite each so that some other element functions as the sentence opener. Use different kinds of elements.

1. The tomb of the first emperor of China was unearthed on Mount Li in Shensi, China, in 1974.

2. Archaeologists discovered an amazing collection of more than seven thousand clay soldiers and real weapons.

3. They all made up a huge army that apparently was supposed to guard the body of the emperor and testify to his glory.

4. The site consisted of four pits, one of which contained an enormous military formation.

5. The second pit held chariots, horses, and warriors, while the third pit was the headquarters for the "army" and the final pit was empty.

6. This archaeological find revealed to scholars a great deal about the culture that created it.

7. The type of armor worn by the clay soldiers, for example, suggests the behavior of the actual troops in battle.

8. The weapons uncovered were still dangerously sharp, another sign of the military might of the dynasty.

9. Surviving records indicate that the emperor, who was obviously interested in fame, planned the tomb himself and had it built by more than seven hundred thousand workers.

10. His dynasty dissolved soon after he died in 201 B.C., but his tomb remains a monument to his powerful rule.

Chapter 8

Exercise 10 Varying Sentence Length and Openers

Most of the following sentences are of about the same length, and all begin with the subject. Rewrite the paragraph to increase variety in sentence structure and length.

Napoléon Bonaparte was sent to Egypt in 1798. He intended to build a canal across the Suez Isthmus. His surveyors believed that the Red Sea was thirty-two and a half feet higher than the Mediterranean. They were mistaken, so they decided to abandon the project. An international survey was conducted in the late 1830s. The survey discovered the two bodies of water to be approximately level. This discovery led a French promoter, Ferdinand de Lesseps, to seek the canal concession from the viceroy of Egypt. This promoter raised money from French investors. The viceroy provided conscripted labor. Laborers were also imported from Italy, France, and the Balkans. The Suez Canal finally opened on November 17, 1869. The opening was accompanied by great ceremony and celebration.

Chapter

9 *Words*

An important part of becoming a good writer is developing a genuine curiosity about words.

1. Using the Dictionary

Unabridged dictionaries are comprehensive guides to the language. They typically trace not only the origins of each word but also the history of its usage. Abridged, or condensed, dictionaries provide a selection of the information contained in their unabridged counterparts. An unabridged dictionary is adequate for almost all writing tasks.

Levels of usage

A good dictionary tells you the contexts in which the use of a word is appropriate, its customary usage. **Standard English** includes the great majority of words and constructions that native speakers would recognize as acceptable in any context, whether spoken or written. Many other words that have a more limited use are labeled in the dictionary in various ways. Words used in only certain sections of the country are labeled *Regional* or *Dialectal*. Other labels—*Archaic, Obsolete,* and *Rare*—identify words that are not in common use. Some words and phrases are associated only with certain groups, whether ethnic, professional, generational, or economic. Dictionaries use special terms, discussed below, to distinguish such words from Standard English. Appropriateness also depends on level of formality; many constructions are acceptable in informal contexts but not in formal ones.

    Edited English is relatively formal Standard English. It is defined not only by choice of words but also by conventions of spelling, punctuation, grammatical usage, and sentence structure. The general subject of this book is Edited English.

    Formal English appears in scholarly articles, formal speeches, official documents, and other contexts calling for careful attention to propriety. It also includes specialized, technical vocabularies.

    Colloquial English is conversational English, the casual, relaxed language that we use with friends.

    Regional English often includes words that are standard in speech but should be avoided for general public writing.

Dialects are varieties of language spoken in a particular region or by a socially identifiable group of people. These words and constructions are often labeled *Nonstandard*. Although they are expressive varieties of English, they are inappropriate in Edited English. *Nonstandard* is also used to indicate misspellings, unconventional punctuation, and even widespread usages not acceptable in Edited English.

Slang is the label given to words with a forced, exaggerated, or humorous meaning used in extremely informal contexts. Slang goes out of fashion very quickly. It should almost never be used in Edited English.

Chapter 9

Exercise 1 Using the Dictionary: Definitions

After looking up the following words in your dictionary, write sentences that clearly illustrate the meaning of each word.

1. hegemony

2. repacious

3. soporific

4. exacerbate

5. predilection

6. ebullient

7. mundane

8. officious

9. misogynist

10. abrogate

Chapter 9

Exercise 2 Using the Dictionary: Abbreviations

Look up the following abbreviations in your dictionary, and write down the meaning of each.

1. N.B.

2. cf.

3. RFD

4. WHO

5. DST

6. OE

7. Man.

8. MS

9. HRH

10. et al.

Chapter 9

Exercise 3 Using the Dictionary: Using Words Precisely

Look up the meaning of each word in the following groups. For each word, write a sentence that clearly illustrates how its meaning differs from that of the other words in the group.

1. brief
   terse
   succinct

2. entreat
   order
   request

3. incensed
   annoyed
   perturbed

4. pause
   hesitate
   desist

5. protagonist
   hero
   champion

6. destroy
   decimate
   desecrate

Chapter 9

Exercise 4   Using Words Appropriately

In the following sentences, underline the more appropriate word in each pair. Then write a sentence using the other word appropriately.

1. Fortunately, the foolish agreement I made with my landlord was just (oral/ verbal), not written.

2. Dean Johnson is (currently/presently) in a meeting, but she will be available soon.

3. While we were away on vacation, our home was (burglarized/robbed).

4. Robert's feelings about what major to declare in college (oscillate/vacillate), depending on which class he has just attended.

5. The woman sitting (beside/besides) me spilled her coffee on my notebook.

6. My grandfather (emigrated/immigrated) from Norway when he was twenty years old.

7. The defendant was found guilty of committing the (amoral/immoral) act.

8. After eating at the roadside diner, I felt (nauseated/nauseous).

9. The amount of money Mary earned during winter break was (negligent/ negligible), compared with the total she needed for her trip to Europe.

10. The rules of the university (prescribe/proscribe) that incoming freshmen must attend the orientation session.

Chapter 9

Exercise 5 Levels of Usage

With the assistance of a dictionary, underline the word in each pair that best represents formal Standard English.

1. I realized as soon as I arrived at the party that I should (have/of) (gone/went) to the movies instead.
2. Even when I first received the invitation, I was not very (enthused/enthusiastic) about attending.
3. (Irregardless/Regardless), I thought I would try (and/to) have a good time.
4. As I walked in, I (could/couldn't) hardly believe what I saw.
5. I was (real/really) surprised to see what my friends were doing.
6. I knew that if I did not leave quickly, I was (liable/likely) to get into trouble.
7. Turning to my date, I said, "(Let's/Let's us) leave right now."
8. As soon as I walked out the door, I felt (all right/alright), but the experience (impacted on/affected) me deeply.
9. Next time (I hope I will/I hopefully will) follow my instincts.

Chapter 9

Exercise 6 Levels of Usage

For each of the following words, supply an equivalent word from the other two categories.

Formal	Informal	Slang
1. impoverished		
2.	car	
3. odorific		
4.		split, beat it
5.	child	
6.		stuffed (with food)
7.	meal	

Chapter 9

Exercise 7 Levels of Usage: Slang

Because they are so commonly used in speech, the following words may seem appropriate for formal writing but are actually colloquial. Write a sentence using each. Then rewrite the sentence using a more formal equivalent for the word. Did you have to change other elements of the sentence to make the second version sound more formal?

1. guy

2. hassle

3. spaced-out

4. cop-out

5. burned-out (or wiped out)

10   *Revising the Essay*

1. Understanding Revision

Revision is "seeing again"—the chance to rethink an argument, reconsider evidence, rearrange ideas, rephrase sentences. Although you may revise as you compose, you also need to take time after completing a draft to review what you have produced.

a. Recognize the two types of revision

Macrorevision involves the larger elements that make an essay successful: the sharpness of its focus, the clarity of its organization, and the appropriateness and specificity of its supporting evidence.

    Microrevision involves smaller changes, like those ensuring that sentences are clear and concise, diction is specific, and punctuation is correct.

    This chapter and the next will focus on macrorevision; Chapters 12 and 13, on microrevision. Actually, however, most writers constantly move back and forth between larger and smaller elements as they revise their work.

b. Leave time after finishing a draft before you revise

When possible, allow some time—at least a few hours, preferably a few days—to elapse between drafting an essay and revising it. Returning to an essay after such a break will help you see your work more objectively.

c. Analyze your draft systematically

Using a revision checklist—such as the one printed inside the back cover of *The Heath Handbook* or the Peer Editing Worksheet printed in Exercise 1—can help you to analyze a draft one element at a time.

d. Be open to possible changes in your draft

Genuine revision requires that you be willing to let go of lines, passages, or perhaps even pages that took you hours to put down on paper. The advice and suggestions of both your instructor and your peers can help you find new ways of seeing your paper. In addition, your responses to the work of your peers can enable them to see their work through different eyes.

Chapter 10

Exercise 1 Revising an Essay

Using the Peer Editing Worksheet that follows, evaluate the student paper below. Be thorough, but also use a tone that you think would be helpful to a peer.

Aloha

1   I find it sad that so often words with originally serious meanings become the slang so lightly used in our everyday language. Take, for example, the Hawaiian word *aloha*. Today, *aloha* is a chic way for saying "hello," especially around the little beach towns in Southern California. Used in other contexts, it sometimes means nothing more than "Hawaiian." *Aloha* has also become a meaningless word that tourists in Hawaii proclaim, not knowing its meaning, but thrilled that they know (but cannot pronounce) a Hawaiian word. *Aloha* has become a fun word, an empty expression, but to the people of Hawaii it is a warm, friendly, sincere word that includes a multiplicity of feelings.

2   *Aloha* in Hawaiian is a term of endearment. Although there is no equivalent English meaning, the closest and most accurate English translation would be "love." *To give someone your aloha* is to give them your deepest, heartfelt feelings of "best wishes and love." Many times you will hear someone say, "My aloha goes out to you." You know that you are someone special and dear if this is said to you, for *aloha* embraces strong feelings. The term is not used lightly, but expresses the most sincere feelings of the heart.

3   *Aloha* used in a different context comes close to the English words *blessing* and *consent*. For example, when a couple decides to get married, their parents will either give their aloha, or will oppose the marriage. If the parents give their aloha, they give the couple their blessing by opening up their hearts to the event.

4   *Aloha* in Hawaiian is also a term of appreciation, much like *thank you* in English. When someone does something nice that you greatly appreciate, you might send them a card expressing your aloha, in the same way that someone sends you a thank-you note.

5   In conjunction with being the Hawaiian term for "morning," "afternoon," and "night," *aloha* also becomes a greeting. If a friend says "Aloha kakahiaka" to you, he or she is saying "Good morning." Paradoxically, *aloha* is also a salutation. You would use it the same way that you use *sincerely* to close a letter, or say "good-bye" when leaving people behind. Often, I end my letters with *aloha,* or a phrase like *much love and aloha.* Used as "good-bye," *aloha* means that you are leaving a little of your love with the person. In other contexts, it can show gratitude. Queen Liliuokalani expressed both her love and her gratitude when, on the eve of the annexation of the Hawaiian Islands, she wrote the song "Aloha Oe." It expresses her love for the islands and their people, her gratitude for so much, as well as her sorrow at the overthrow of the monarchy. The song was her farewell address, her last aloha to the people of Hawaii.

6   The multiplicity and complexity of *aloha*'s meanings make it a difficult word to define, for in no other language is there a word completely or closely synonymous to *aloha*. It seems that to truly understand its meaning, you must grow up learning it and feeling it. The word should not be used as slang, for it loses the beauty of its meaning that is so special and dear to the Hawaiian people. It should be used sincerely, seriously, warmly. I hate to hear it abused.

Peer Editing Worksheet

1. What does this paper's introduction accomplish? Does it introduce the writer's subject? Does it arouse your interest in the paper?

2. What is the thesis statement in this paper?

3. Briefly state the paper's main points, and then comment on how effectively each of these points supports the paper's thesis.

Paragraph 1

Main point:

Support:

Paragraph 2
Main point:

Support:

Paragraph 3
Main point:

Support:

Paragraph 4
Main point:

Support:

Paragraph 5

Main point:

Support:

Paragraph 6

Main point:

Support:

4. If you were writing this paper, what other points might you use to support its thesis?

5. Identify the most successful paragraph and the least successful paragraph of the paper, and explain why you selected them. Consider such matters as the following: Is the paragraph's main idea clearly indicated? Is the paragraph's development effective? Is the organization easy to follow?

Most successful paragraph
Reasons:

Least successful paragraph

Reasons:

6. Identify two or three of the strongest sentences in the paper, and explain why you selected each (for example, vivid diction, effective use of parallel structure, good sense of the writer's voice). Give the paragraph number and the sentence number.

Strongest sentences

(a) _____

Reasons:

(b) ——————————

Reasons:

(c) ——————————

Reasons:

7. Identify two or three of the weakest sentences in the paper, and explain why you selected each (for example, confusing syntax, vague diction, awkward phrasing, wordiness). Give the paragraph number and the sentence number.

Weakest sentences

(a) _____

Reasons:

(b) _____

Reasons:

(c) _____

Reasons:

8. What does the paper's conclusion accomplish? Does it bring the paper to a strong close?

11

Revising
Paragraphs

The two most common weaknesses in paragraphs are inadequate development and lack of coherence.

1. Inadequate Development

Although its central idea may be clear, an underdeveloped paragraph is too brief, general, thin, or dull. Developing a paragraph does not mean padding out a simple statement or repeating the same idea in different words. It means taking time to be clear, accurate, and specific.

a. Recognizing vagueness and generalities

Review your paragraphs for vague, abstract descriptions, such as "very interesting" and "very rewarding." Even if the ideas are clear to you, you need to be specific in relating them to your readers.

b. Using concrete diction and specific detail

Specific detail comes from recalling the taste, touch, sound, and sight of an event as precisely as possible, providing your readers with the information they need to picture it. It's the choice of words, not the number of words, that counts.

Vague original

Though the air was uncomfortable, the sand was nice, and I dug a hole into it and piled it up until it half-covered me from the air. I rested for a while and watched the sea rise and fall and the various objects it threw onto the beach. Seaweed and other things were washed up, then carried back in a regular rhythm.

Revised for detail

Though the air was cold, the sand felt soft and warm, and I dug a damp trough in it and piled it up around my legs until I had a body only from the waist up. Later I rested my head on my knees and watched the sea rise and fall, bringing with it to the beach something new each time: a loop of rust-colored seaweed, a shell, a rock, a small jellyfish. And falling away, it would often take with it what it had just brought.

Keep in mind that to develop a paragraph, you do not have to pack it with elaborate descriptions. Choose from the details at hand those which will best support your main point.

2. Lack of Coherence

Within every paragraph, arrange and link the sentences so that your readers can easily follow your point. Your readers must see how each sentence is related to the one that precedes it and how it leads into the one that comes next. Items a–d below will help you achieve coherence.

a. Transitional words

Using transitional words and phrases will make your paragraphs more coherent. Be careful not to overuse them, though, and don't always use them in the same place (for example, as the first word in a sentence). Also be careful to use the precise one you need.

Cause or Effect

as a result	since
because	so
consequently	therefore
hence	thus

Comparison or Contrast

in the same way	in contrast
likewise	nonetheless
similarly	on the contrary
	on the other hand
but	still
however	yet

Example

for example	specifically
for instance	

Addition

also	moreover
besides	next
furthermore	too
in addition	

Conclusion

in conclusion	to conclude
in short	to sum up

b. Linking pronouns

You may also connect sentences by pronouns that have clear antecedents. This technique is an effective way of avoiding needless repetition. However, when you use a word like *it* or *him* or *them,* make sure that its antecedent—the word you've used earlier that it refers to—is unmistakable to your readers.

c. Repetition of key words

The repetition of key words that are related to a central idea will help you maintain paragraph coherence.

d. Parallel structure

Parallel structure calls attention to similar ideas. Beginning several sentences in a row with the same subject, for example, can emphasize your point. Use this technique consciously and sparingly.

e. Maintaining coherence between paragraphs

The primary devices for maintaining coherence between paragraphs are the same as those for providing coherence within a paragraph. Equally important is the arrangement of the material so that a paragraph begins with some reference to the idea that has preceded it and its relationship to the one that will follow. Do not just repeat part of the last sentence of the preceding paragraph or begin with *in addition;* work to find more subtle transitions.

All of these devices for creating coherence will be effective only if the ideas in your writing are closely and logically connected.

Chapter 11

Exercise 1 Concrete Diction and Specific Detail

The following is an undeveloped paragraph full of generalities and vague diction. Revise the passage to eliminate both problems. Begin by listing as many concrete examples or details as you can. Then decide which seem the most effective, and write the new paragraph. If you choose, base your revision on personal experience to make the points more vivid.

> There are many very important reasons why a child should have a pet. First, a pet can be a playmate when adults or other children are not available. In addition, by caring for a pet's needs, a child can learn the meaning of responsibility. Finally, taking care of a pet teaches a child a great deal about the value of affection. Everyone should have the opportunity to own some kind of pet.

Chapter 11

Exercise 2 Paragraph Coherence: Transitional Words

Underline the transitional words used to create coherence in the following passage.

Ignored by most American tourists hurrying to Florence, Venice, or Rome, Bologna is the lovely, historical capital of the Emilia Romagna region of Italy. Many travelers have passed through its main train station, Bologna Centrale, since the city is at the crossroads of several railway lines and in the center of northern Italy. However, most passengers head elsewhere: to Venice 80 miles northeast of it, to Florence 45 miles south, to Genoa 120 miles west, or to Milan 150 miles northwest. Because they choose these other destinations, these tourists miss the special culture, beauty, and history that cannot be found anywhere but in Bologna.

Bologna, at the base of the northern Appenines, was founded by Romans in the second century B.C. on what was once an ancient Etruscan settlement. Like many medieval towns, Bologna was walled to protect the city; but unlike those in many Italian cities, the gates and parts of Bologna's walls remain intact. Other forms of defense, too, became signatures of the city. For example, in the old sections the sidewalks are spanned by huge porticoes, once designed to protect buildings from foot soldiers or mounted attack and today used to protect pedestrians from the elements. Few homes in the older parts of town open to the street; instead, they look out over courtyards hidden from public view—and at one time from invasion—by walls several stories high. In the center of town, the two towers were, in the twelfth century, lookout posts from which guards could watch the progress of enemies through the valley. Now, closed to the public, the towers watch over the city, reminders of a more aggressive era.

Bologna has always been a cultural center: its university, founded in 1088 and one of the oldest in Europe, has always attracted scholars. Specifically, Galvani, who discovered electrical current, and Malpighi, who discovered capillaries, taught

at it. Today, the University of Bologna maintains schools of law, medicine, and veterinary medicine, besides its liberal arts and science programs. Bologna also has an important collection of art, including Etruscan relics and frescoes by the Bolognese master Correggio.

In addition to its culture and history, Bologna is interesting in terms of politics. The city has maintained an independent air, politically. It was an independent state until 1506, when it was incorporated into the Papal States by Julius II. In 1860, Bologna was made part of the Kingdom of Italy. Furthermore, it was a center of the resistance during World War II. During the war, the Fascisti captured a number of Partigiani (underground partisans) in the city. The resistance workers were shot; as a result, a memorial, which includes photographs of the victims, now stands in the city's main square. Today, Bologna is the center of the Italian Communist Party (CPI), which is a moderate party by Italian standards and is not aligned with Moscow, Beijing, or other Communist governments.

Chapter 11

Exercise 3 Paragraph Coherence: Linking Pronouns

Underline the linking pronouns in the following passage.

Ignored by most American tourists hurrying to Florence, Venice, or Rome, Bologna is the lovely, historical capital of the Emilia Romagna region of Italy. Many travelers have passed through its main train station, Bologna Centrale, since the city is at the crossroads of several railway lines and in the center of northern Italy. However, most passengers head elsewhere: to Venice 80 miles northeast of it, to Florence 45 miles south, to Genoa 120 miles west, or to Milan 150 miles northwest. Because they choose these other destinations, these tourists miss the special culture, beauty, and history that cannot be found anywhere but in Bologna.

Bologna, at the base of the northern Appenines, was founded by Romans in the second century B.C. on what was once an ancient Etruscan settlement. Like many medieval towns, Bologna was walled to protect the city; but unlike those in many Italian cities, the gates and parts of Bologna's walls remain intact. Other forms of defense, too, became signatures of the city. For example, in the old sections the sidewalks are spanned by huge porticoes, once designed to protect buildings from foot soldiers or mounted attack and today used to protect pedestrians from the elements. Few homes in the older parts of town open to the street; instead, they look out over courtyards hidden from public view—and at one time from invasion—by walls several stories high. In the center of town, the two towers were, in the twelfth century, lookout posts from which guards could watch the progress of enemies through the valley. Now, closed to the public, the towers watch over the city, reminders of a more aggressive era.

Bologna has always been a cultural center: its university, founded in 1088 and one of the oldest in Europe, has always attracted scholars. Specifically, Galvani, who discovered electrical current, and Malpighi, who discovered capillaries, taught

at it. Today, the University of Bologna maintains schools of law, medicine, and veterinary medicine, besides its liberal arts and science programs. Bologna also has an important collection of art, including Etruscan relics and frescoes by the Bolognese master Correggio.

In addition to its culture and history, Bologna is interesting in terms of politics. The city has maintained an independent air, politically. It was an independent state until 1506, when it was incorporated into the Papal States by Julius II. In 1860, Bologna was made part of the Kingdom of Italy. Furthermore, it was a center of the resistance during World War II. During the war, the Fascisti captured a number of Partigiani (underground partisans) in the city. The resistance workers were shot; as a result, a memorial, which includes photographs of the victims, now stands in the city's main square. Today, Bologna is the center of the Italian Communist Party (CPI), which is a moderate party by Italian standards and is not aligned with Moscow, Beijing, or other Communist governments.

Chapter 11

Exercise 4 Paragraph Coherence: Parallel Structure

Underline the parallel structures in the following passage.

Ignored by most American tourists hurrying to Florence, Venice, or Rome, Bologna is the lovely, historical capital of the Emilia Romagna region of Italy. Many travelers have passed through its main train station, Bologna Centrale, since the city is at the crossroads of several railway lines and in the center of northern Italy. However, most passengers head elsewhere: to Venice 80 miles northeast of it, to Florence 45 miles south, to Genoa 120 miles west, or to Milan 150 miles northwest. Because they choose these other destinations, these tourists miss the special culture, beauty, and history that cannot be found anywhere but in Bologna.

Bologna, at the base of the northern Appenines, was founded by Romans in the second century B.C. on what was once an ancient Etruscan settlement. Like many medieval towns, Bologna was walled to protect the city; but unlike those in many Italian cities, the gates and parts of Bologna's walls remain intact. Other forms of defense, too, became signatures of the city. For example, in the old sections the sidewalks are spanned by huge porticoes, once designed to protect buildings from foot soldiers or mounted attack and today used to protect pedestrians from the elements. Few homes in the older parts of town open to the street; instead, they look out over courtyards hidden from public view—and at one time from invasion—by walls several stories high. In the center of town, the two towers were, in the twelfth century, lookout posts from which guards could watch the progress of enemies through the valley. Now, closed to the public, the towers watch over the city, reminders of a more aggressive era.

Bologna has always been a cultural center: its university, founded in 1088 and one of the oldest in Europe, has always attracted scholars. Specifically, Galvani, who discovered electrical current, and Malpighi, who discovered capillaries, taught

at it. Today, the University of Bologna maintains schools of law, medicine, and veterinary medicine, besides its liberal arts and science programs. Bologna also has an important collection of art, including Etruscan relics and frescoes by the Bolognese master Correggio.

In addition to its culture and history, Bologna is interesting in terms of politics. The city has maintained an independent air, politically. It was an independent state until 1506, when it was incorporated into the Papal States by Julius II. In 1860, Bologna was made part of the Kingdom of Italy. Furthermore, it was a center of the resistance during World War II. During the war, the Fascisti captured a number of Partigiani (underground partisans) in the city. The resistance workers were shot; as a result, a memorial, which includes photographs of the victims, now stands in the city's main square. Today, Bologna is the center of the Italian Communist Party (CPI), which is a moderate party by Italian standards and is not aligned with Moscow, Beijing, or other Communist governments.

12 *Revising Sentences*

If you are like most writers, you shape sentences crudely during the preliminary stages of writing because you are trying to maintain the flow of your ideas. Revising demands that you later examine each statement to see if it says exactly what you want it to say. As you reshape your sentences, you also need to pay attention to your diction, the element of revision discussed in Chapter 13.

1. Unclear Pronoun Reference

The noun a pronoun stands for is called the **antecedent** because it usually goes before the pronoun.

antecedent   pronoun
Rita lives in Boulder, but *she* grew up in San Diego.

In some constructions, the antecedent may follow the pronoun.

       pronoun   antecedent
Although *it* was delayed, the *plane* finally took off.

As you revise, make sure that the antecedent of every pronoun is clear.

a. Ambiguous reference

Do not use a pronoun in such a way that it might refer to either of two antecedents.

Unclear	The novelist Virginia Woolf assured her sister Vanessa, who was a painter, that *she* was a great artist. [Does *she* refer to Virginia Woolf or to her sister?]
Correct	The novelist Virginia Woolf told her sister Vanessa, who was a painter, "You are a great artist."
Unclear	In *Nostromo,* Conrad's style is ironic and his setting is highly symbolic, so that *it* sometimes confuses the reader.

Correct	In *Nostromo,* Conrad's style is ironic, and his highly symbolic setting sometimes confuses the reader.

b. Remote reference

A pronoun too far away from its antecedent may cause misreading.

Unclear	By 1890, architects in Chicago had perfected the floating raft foundation, a thick mat of concrete with embedded steel rails that would evenly distribute the weight of a heavy structure. *It* could support a building of sixteen or more tons.

Either repeat the antecedent or recast the sentence.

Correct	By 1890, architects in Chicago had perfected the floating raft foundation, a thick mat of concrete with embedded steel rails that would evenly distribute the weight of a heavy structure. *Such a foundation* could support a building of sixteen or more tons.
Correct	By 1890, architects in Chicago had perfected the floating raft foundation. This thick mat of concrete with embedded steel rails could support a building of sixteen or more tons.

c. Broad pronoun reference: *this, that, which*

Using the pronouns *this, that,* or *which* to refer broadly to the idea of the preceding clause or sentence can confuse your reader.

Unclear	The beginning of the book is more interesting than the conclusion, which is unfortunate. [The pronoun *which* seems to refer

> to *conclusion.* The writer wants
> the *which* to refer to the whole
> idea of the main clause.]

Revise such a sentence to eliminate the pronoun or to give it a definite antecedent.

Correct

Unfortunately, the beginning of the book is more interesting than the conclusion.

Do not use the pronoun *this* alone as the beginning word in a sentence that follows another sentence of great length or complexity.

Unclear

The Japanese fugu is a lethal fish, yet it is considered a choice dish in Tokyo and other cities, where it sells for more than $200 a plate. *This* means that its preparation must be controlled and supervised.

Correct

This toxicity means that its preparation must be controlled and supervised.

d. Indefinite use of *it, they, you*

A number of idiomatic expressions use the impersonal pronoun: *It is hot. It is late.* Avoid, however, the *it* that needs a clear antecedent and has none.

Unclear

Lewis Thomas, author of *Lives of the Cell,* is a physician and writer who spends his spare hours practicing *it.*

Correct

Lewis Thomas, author of *Lives of the Cell,* is a physician who spends his spare hours *writing.*

Also avoid using *they* when it does not have a clear reference.

Unclear

If intercollegiate football were banned, *they* would have to develop an elaborate intramural program.

| Correct | If intercollegiate football were banned, *each college* would have to develop an elaborate intramural program. |

Although the indefinite use of *you* to refer to people in general is widespread, formal usage restricts *you* to mean *"you the reader."*

Informal	Small classes give *you* a chance to take part in discussions.
Formal	Small classes give *one* a chance to take part in discussions.
Formal	Small classes give *the student* a chance to take part in discussions.

2. Dangling Modifiers

A modifier is a word or phrase that functions in a sentence to limit or describe another word or group of words. If there is no word or group of words in the sentence for the modifier to limit or describe, the modifier *dangles*. Almost all dangling modifiers occur at the beginning of a sentence.

| Dangling | *Having waited an hour to digest our food,* the lake felt cool on that hot summer afternoon. |

The literal syntax of this sentence states that the lake, well fed, felt cool. To correct this error, supply the noun or pronoun the phrase should modify.

| Correct | Having waited an hour to digest our food, *we* plunged into the lake, which felt cool on that hot summer afternoon. |

Another solution is to change the dangling modifier into a complete clause.

| Correct | After we had waited an hour to digest our food, the lake felt cool on that hot summer afternoon. |

a. Dangling participial phrases

Participial phrases are verbal modifiers that function in the sentence as adjectives do. When a participial phrase begins a sentence, the word it modifies must immediately follow it.

Dangling	*Analyzing Joan Didion's style, her essay* seemed to me to be cool and detached.
Correct	Analyzing Joan Didion's style, *I* discovered that the writing, especially in this essay, was cool and detached.

b. Dangling gerunds

A gerund is a verb form ending in *-ing* that is used as a noun. A gerund phrase dangles when the subject of the gerund—the actor—is not apparent to the reader.

Dangling	*When doing research, notes* should be entered on separate index cards.
Correct	When doing research, *a writer* should take notes on separate index cards.

c. Dangling infinitives

An infinitive, a verb preceded by the word *to,* dangles when the subject of its action is not expressed. Make clear who is doing the action.

Dangling	*To be considered for law school, the LSAT* must be taken.
Correct	To be considered for law school, *an applicant* must take the LSAT.

d. Dangling elliptical clauses

Sometimes we omit the subject and main verb from a dependent clause: *while going* instead of *while I was going,* or *when a child* instead of *when I was a child.* Such an elliptical construction is correct as long as its subject is clear. If the subject is not absolutely clear, however, the construction dangles.

Dangling	Do not add the beans *until thoroughly soaked.*
Correct	Do not add the beans *until they are thoroughly soaked.*

3. Misplaced Modifiers

A modifier is misplaced if it is not near enough to the word it is intended to modify. Unlike the dangling modifier, which cannot logically modify any word in the sentence, the misplaced modifier may seem to modify the wrong word or phrase in the sentence.

Misplaced	She wrote the full story of her recovery from drug addiction *in only a month.*
Correct	*In only a month,* she wrote the full story of her recovery from drug addiction.

A modifier is said to squint, or to look two ways at once, when it might refer to either a preceding word or a following word in the sentence.

Squinting	The tailback who injured his knee *recently* returned to practice.
Correct	The tailback who *recently* injured his knee returned to practice.
Correct	The tailback who injured his knee returned *recently* to practice.

4. Split Constructions

Avoid splitting the parts of a verb phrase with a long modifying phrase or clause.

Split	I *have,* more than the rest of the class, *been* in a panic since the paper was assigned.

| Correct | More than the rest of the class, I *have been* in a panic since the paper was assigned. |

Split infinitives—infinitives with a modifier between the *to* and the verb—also often seem awkward.

| Split | We found it difficult *to* accurately *describe* the car involved in the accident. |
| Revised | We found it difficult *to describe* accurately the car involved in the accident. |

If eliminating a split infinitive would result in even greater awkwardness, however, let the construction stand.

5. Confusing Shifts

a. Confusing shifts of voice or subject

A shift from the active to the passive voice almost always involves a confusing change in the subject as well.

| Shift | After I finally discovered an unsoldered wire, the dismantling of the motor was begun. |
| Correct | After I finally discovered an unsoldered wire, I began to dismantle the motor. |

b. Confusing shifts of person or number

A shift in person—for example, from the third person (*he, she, one*) to the second person (*you*)—usually results in an unfocused sentence.

Shift	When *one* tries hard enough, *you* can do almost anything.
Correct	When *you* try hard enough, *you* can do almost anything.
Correct	When *people* try hard enough, *they* can do almost anything.

A shift in number from singular to plural confuses the reader and results in faulty pronoun agreement.

Shift	If a *customer* is kept waiting, *they* should complain to the management.
Correct	If *customers* are kept waiting, *they* should complain to the management.

c. Confusing shifts of mood or tense

A sentence should end in the same mood in which it began.

Shift	First, *locate* the library on a campus map; next, *you should find* the card catalog and the reference section. [shift from imperative to indicative]
Correct	First, *locate* the library on a campus map; next, *find* the card catalog and the reference section.

If a sentence begins in the past tense, do not carelessly end it in the present tense.

Shift	I *stood* on the starting block and *looked* tensely at the water below; for the first time in my life I *am* about to swim in competition.
Correct	I *stood* on the starting block and *looked* tensely at the water below; for the first time in my life I *was* about to swim in competition.

6. Mixed constructions

A mixed construction occurs when a sentence that begins with one grammatical construction shifts to another.

Mixed	*By requiring* drivers to have their cars inspected *is one way* to cut down on accidents.
Correct	*Requiring* drivers to have their cars inspected *is one way* to cut down on accidents.

a. Dependent clauses misused as subjects and complements

Using a dependent clause as the subject or the complement of a verb can produce a mixed construction.

Mixed	Because they installed solar heating when they remodeled their house made their fuel bills lower.
Correct	Because they installed solar heating when they remodeled their house, their fuel bills were lower.

b. Adverbial clauses misused as nouns

A common mixed construction is seen in the illogical use of *when* or *where* as part of the complement of *is*—the *is when* or *is where* error.

Mixed	One thing that keeps me from driving to the city *is when* I think of the traffic jams.
Correct	One thing that keeps me from driving to the city *is the thought of* the traffic jams.
Correct	The thought of the traffic jams keeps me from driving to the city.
Mixed	Symbiosis *is where* dissimilar organisms live together in a mutually advantageous partnership.
Correct	Symbiosis is *a state in which* dissimilar organisms live together in a mutually advantageous partnership.

| Correct | Symbiosis *is* the mutually advantageous partnership of dissimilar organisms. |

c. Unidiomatic comparisons

Be careful not to mix idiomatic ways of making comparisons.

| Mixed | Erasable paper is easier *to type on than on bond.* |
| Correct | Erasable paper is easier *to type on than bond is.* |

7. Incomplete Constructions

Do not omit words necessary for grammatical completeness, particularly in compound constructions.

a. Incomplete verb forms

When both verbs in a compound construction are in the same tense, the second auxiliary verb can be omitted.

> Information will be sent to all students who *have registered* for the Education Abroad program and [who have] *paid* the fee.

When the verbs in a compound construction are in different tenses, write both out in full.

| Incomplete | Modern languages *have* and always *will be* an important part of the curriculum. |
| Correct | Modern languages *have been* and always *will be* an important part of the curriculum. |

b. Omitted prepositions

When the verbs or adjectives in a compound construction take different prepositions, include both.

| Incomplete | He was *oblivious* and *undisturbed by* the noise around him. |

Correct	He was *oblivious to* and *undisturbed by* the noise around him.

c. Incomplete comparisons

In comparisons, do not omit words necessary to make a complete idiomatic statement.

Incomplete	She is *as witty*, if not wittier *than,* her brother.
Correct	She is *as witty as,* if not wittier *than,* her brother.

Avoid the illogical use of *any* and *than.*

Incomplete	For many years the Empire State Building was taller than *any* building in New York.
Correct	For many years the Empire State Building was taller than *any other* building in New York.

Make sure the reader can tell what is being compared with what.

Incomplete	Claremont is further from Los Angeles *than* Pomona.
Correct	Claremont is further from Los Angeles *than* Pomona *is.*

Chapter *12*

Exercise 1 Unclear Pronoun Reference

Revise the following sentences to correct unclear pronoun reference.

1. In the distant past, they believed that left-handed people were sinister.

2. This comes from the roots of the word *left*.

3. Not long ago, a mother might have convinced her daughter that she preferred using her right hand, even if she really were left-handed.

4. Teachers forced left-handed students to write their way and adapt to them.

5. Although attitudes have changed, it is still a problem.

6. Guitarists who play left-handed, for example, are at a disadvantage, because they need to be braced and strung differently.

7. Even though 10 percent of the population is left-handed, people often notice others using their left hands, who then sometimes feel self-conscious.

8. Specialty stores offer items for left-handers, but they are often inconvenient.

9. More males than females are left-handed, and more native Americans than in the population at large. The reason for this is unknown.

10. Despite the difficulties, a great number of left-handers have achieved fame, such as Charlie Chaplin and Pablo Picasso. He is a particularly notable example because he was so creative.

Chapter 12

Exercise 2 Unclear Pronoun Reference

Revise the following sentences to correct unclear pronoun reference.

1. Although they sell many packaged brownie mixes on supermarket shelves, they can easily be made from scratch at home even if you are an inexperienced cook.

2. Begin by measuring out 16 tablespoons of powdered cocoa and melt it with 2 sticks of margarine, either in a microwave oven or on a burner, which work equally well. It does not have to be too precise.

3. If you use a burner, stir it to keep it from sticking.

4. While this cools slightly, stir together 2 cups of sugar and 4 eggs until smooth, and add 2 teaspoons of vanilla. They do not have to be beaten first.

5. Next, add in 1½ cups of flour, blend well, and stir in the cocoa mixture. This should be slightly cool.

6. You'll need an oblong baking pan, 9 by 12 inches, which one should grease with margarine and dust with flour to prevent them from sticking.

7. Pour in the batter and place it into an oven that has been preheated to 300 degrees.

8. The secret to these brownies is keeping them moist, almost like fudge, by checking them and not overcooking them, so do this after about 25 minutes.

9. To check them, insert a toothpick into the middle of the pan; it should seem somewhere between clean and slightly sticky.

10. When they are done, your guests will be impressed by your product, so you will want to serve them again.

Chapter *12*

Exercise 3 Dangling and Misplaced Modifiers, Split Constructions

Rewrite the following sentences to eliminate all dangling modifiers, misplaced modifiers, and split constructions.

1. The first woman to fly solo across the Atlantic Ocean, the world will long remember Amelia Earhart.

2. Earhart's career ended abruptly with her disappearance over the Pacific on July 3, 1937, on her last journey, a twenty-seven-thousand-mile trip around the world, after setting many world records between 1922 and then.

3. Upon searching for three weeks, no clues turned up.

4. Yet because of her popularity and the public's curiosity, her story continued only from that point.

5. While stationed in Saipan in the Pacific, evidence was in 1944 found by military personnel that Earhart and her companion, Frederick Noonan, had crashed there and been then captured by the Japanese.

6. However, this evidence later disappeared, upon trying to follow up on her story.

7. In the 1960s and 1970s, a number of books and articles hypothesized that Earhart indeed was doing surveillance work for the U.S. government and that the information about her death was, by government officials, intentionally covered up.

8. Despite lacking solid proof, speculation continues about this remarkable woman, a mystery perhaps never to be solved.

9. Before flying for the last time, newspapers reported that Earhart said, "Women must try to do things as men have tried; when they fail, their failure must be a challenge to others."

10. Although a failure, a courageous example for both women and men lives on in Earhart's story.

Chapter *12*

Exercise 4 Dangling and Misplaced Modifiers, Split Constructions

Rewrite the following sentences to eliminate all dangling modifiers, misplaced modifiers, and split constructions.

1. Hovering above, we may not have noticed them as we shopped on a busy city street, or perhaps we were concentrating too hard to see them as we toured a church or a college campus.

2. Nonetheless, they were there, silent, still, and watching us, the stony figurines that decorate buildings in every part of our cities, gargoyles and grotesques.

3. With the specific architectural purpose of serving as waterspouts, the ancient Greeks designed gargoyles to protect buildings from damage from rain by directing the water away from the building.

4. First designed in the shape of a lion's head, masons later sculpted the figures in a variety of shapes.

5. In medieval times, builders carved gargoyles to, as a sort of architectural satire, resemble political figures.

6. In the Elizabethan era, architects, in the shape of divine, peaceful women, made the figures more pastoral.

7. Today, the statuettes are in all manner of humans and beasts designed.

8. However, after finding more practical ways of preventing structural damage from rain and snow, the carvings that adorn buildings today are spoutless.

9. These spoutless gargoyles are called grotesques by engineers, a name that does not express their beauty.

10. Walking downtown, passing a church, or strolling across campus, stone faces are all around us and are worth appreciating.

Chapter 12

Exercise 5 *Confusing Shifts*

Revise the following sentences to correct shifts in voice or subject, person or number, and mood or tense.

1. Rummage sales, also called garage sales, can be fun to visit—you never know what bargains you would find.

2. Dedicated rummagers should check the newspaper listings the night before, and then you can show up at the very start.

3. Although some people even come early and wait around, hoping to get a head start, sellers usually discouraged this practice.

4. Even if you don't find anything you need at a rummage sale, we all are entertained by what other people think is worth spending money on.

5. Many customers like to haggle about prices; usually this technique is found worthwhile by them.

6. However, be careful not to insult the owner by offering a low bid on what they believed was a family heirloom.

7. You might also decide to return to a sale later in the day, because if the item is still there, one might get it for a lower price.

8. Sometimes, of course, a person might take home an item that will just clutter up the house until the next time you have a garage sale of your own.

Chapter *12*

Exercise 6 Mixed and Incomplete Constructions

Correct the mixed and incomplete constructions in the following sentences.

1. On January 10, 1962, at 6:00 P.M., the Peruvian towns and villages in the shade of Nevado Huascaron, the twenty-two-thousand-foot mountain in the Andes range of Peru, were as quiet if not quieter than they usually were.

2. The valley below, called the Callejon de Huailas, was home to thousands of people who depended and looked to the mountain for their livelihood.

3. These residents were unaware and unprepared for a disaster.

4. One thing that might have warned residents was where the heavy snows had been followed by exceptionally warm weather.

5. Because the thaw created rivers in the ice weakened its grasp on the steep slope.

6. At 6:13 P.M., when Glacier 511 shifted and strained against the northwestern slope of the mountain began the avalanche.

7. The reason the villagers received no warning was when the avalanche of three million tons of ice, snow, and debris moved quietly at first.

8. By collecting mud and rocks along its route is one way the avalanche picked up speed.

9. It thundered down the slopes through the towns, leaving a devastation of rubble and debris worse than that of any natural disaster in that area.

10. Although the barrage of ice and rock plunged into a river did not stop the damage from continuing; the river dammed and flooded the plains beyond the valley.

11. Just because the avalanche lasted only seven minutes did not mean it was harmless.

12. The disaster destroyed eight villages and killed at least as many if not more than thirty-five hundred people.

Chapter *12*

Exercise 7 Mixed and Incomplete Constructions

Correct the mixed and incomplete constructions in the following sentences.

1. Australia is the home of many strange animals, but the kangaroo is more remarkable than any of them.

2. That kangaroos are specifically built for jumping is where they are so remarkable.

3. By using their strong back legs and feet to propel themselves in jumps seven feet high and twenty-five feet long is how kangaroos can travel up to forty miles per hour.

4. Because kangaroos are marsupials means that babies, called joeys, are carried in their mothers' pouches, where they spend their first four months tucked safely away, cared and protected by their mothers.

5. Nonetheless, all through their lives kangaroos are in greater danger.

6. Wild dogs have and always will find kangaroos a delicious target, and starvation and thirst often threaten the herd.

7. Ranchers and poachers present to the kangaroos a threat as great if not greater than other animals, and companies even sell kangaroo meat as dog food.

8. Ignoble uses of Australia's most easily identifiable symbol are when the Australian government was prompted to protect the kangaroo.

9. Just because such legislation is in place does not ensure that all kangaroos will jump safely in the wild, but the laws should help.

13   *Revising Diction*

1. Experiencing Words

Language is a link between self and other: in playing with language, we experience the world; in sharpening our words, we make the world manageable. The more fully you understand the ways in which words name the features of the world, the more precise and effective your diction can be. Work on selecting words that most nearly approximate your thoughts and feelings. Begin by looking up the meanings (and pronunciation) of unfamiliar words you come across and familiar ones you cannot define. Keep a vocabulary notebook, and try these words out from time to time in writing and conversation.

2. Denotation and Connotation

Denotations are the most literal meanings of words. Connotations, on the other hand, are a word's overtones, echoes, emotional colorings, and associations.

a. Importance of context

Although the denotations of various words may be similar, the connotation of each word must be appropriate to the context. For example, *to compliment* is used in the context of generous, justified praise given freely. In contrast, *to apple-polish* unmistakably implies blatant insincerity and favor seeking. Other words may have more subtle connotations. Work to become aware of them as you revise.

b. Value of a dictionary

At times you will need to use a good dictionary to determine the precise denotations and connotations of a word.

3. Abstract and Concrete
a. Ladder of abstraction

The second of the complex ways that words name is by their abstractness and their concreteness. Words that name specific, tangible things are **con-**

crete: *enchiladas, elms*. Words that designate general qualities, categories, or relationships are **abstract:** *food, trees*. As the linguist S. I. Hayakawa demonstrated with his "ladder of abstraction," a concrete subject can be thought of at increasing levels of abstraction. While abstract terms are both necessary and useful, at some point they have to be given the substance of concreteness.

b. Value of concrete diction

While the best writing moves gracefully from abstract to concrete and from particular to general, an overdependence on colorless abstractions will make your writing tedious.

Abstract	For dinner we had some really good food.
Concrete	For dinner we had spinach lasagna and marinated vegetables.
Abstract	She likes to argue about controversial subjects.
Concrete	She likes to argue about welfare reform and socialized medicine.

When you examine your diction, remember that a specific statement often requires no more space than a vague one does, yet it communicates much more information.

4. Idiom

An **idiom** is an expression peculiar to itself within a language, not explainable by the ordinary meaning of its individual words: *make out* (succeed), *make up* (reconcile), *make do* (be satisfied with). In English we often rely on prepositions to indicate subtle but essential relationships: to take a stand *on* an issue, to be *in* a quandary, to be *out* of luck. Here are a few other idiomatic uses of prepositions:

agree *with* a person, *to* a proposal, *on* a procedure
argue *with* a person, *for* or *about* a measure
differ *from* one another in appearance, differ *with* a person in opinion
independent *of*
stand *by* a friend, *for* a cause, *on* an issue

Idiom demands that certain words be followed by infinitives, others by gerunds.

> Infinitive: able to go, like to go, eager to go
> Gerund: capable of going, enjoy going, cannot help going

Consult a dictionary if you are uncertain whether you have used an idiom correctly.

5. Figurative Language

The right figure of speech can turn an otherwise uninteresting phrase into an original observation.

a. Metaphor and simile

A metaphor is a direct comparison of two things on the basis of a shared quality: All the world's *a stage;* snow *blanketed* the ground; she is at *the peak* of her fame. Make a practice of looking for metaphors not only in nouns (the *heart* of the subject) but also in verbs.

Like a metaphor, a simile states a comparison, but unlike a metaphor, it uses the words *like* or *as* to do so.

> I sensed a wrongness about me, *like* an alarm clock that has gone off without being set.
>
> —Maya Angelou

6. Special Problems of Diction
a. Sexist language

One of the most important changes to occur recently in English is an increased sensitivity to sexist language—usages that treat men and women unequally or that betray stereotypes. Language that refers to women and men should be *inclusive* rather than *exclusive*. If you are not alert to sexist language in your writing, you increasingly run the risk of alienating your readers.

Avoid using man *in a generic sense*

Some writers attempt to defend the traditional use of the word *man* to mean "all human beings" by arguing that its connotation is generic, that it suggests not individual men but people in general: *the average man* or *every man for himself.* This notion is easy to disprove. Consider a sentence like the following:

> On this campus, any man who wants an active social life has to be a member of a fraternity or sorority.

The ending is startling precisely because we do not read the word *man* in the beginning of the sentence in a generic sense, but instead attach to it a male connotation that subsequently clashes with *sorority.* A number of alternatives are available, depending on your meaning:

> On this campus, any man who wants an active social life has to be a member of a fraternity.

> On this campus, any woman who wants an active social life has to be a member of a sorority.

> On this campus, any student who wants an active social life has to be a member of a fraternity or a sorority.

For *man,* substitute *person* or *human being* or whatever noun fits the context. For *mankind,* use *humanity* or *human beings.* The same principle applies to compounds with the word *man.* A gender-neutral substitute is always available: for *man-made,* use *synthetic;* for *manpower,* use *work force.* Finally, also avoid using *man* as a verb:

Exclusive	Representatives of the senior class will *man* the information booth.
Inclusive	Representatives of the senior class will *staff* the information booth.

Avoid using the pronoun he in a generic sense

Like *man,* the pronoun *he* (along with *his, him,* and *himself*) has often been used to refer to people in general when its antecedent is indefinite. However, these personal pronouns *define* their contexts as exclusively male.

Exclusive	Every attorney in the firm understood *himself* and *his* colleagues better after the meeting.

Simply substitute *he or she.* When that alternative seems awkward, recast the sentence using plural nouns and pronouns.

Inclusive	*All the attorneys* in the firm understood *themselves* and *their* colleagues better after the meeting.

Use gender-neutral language to identify people's roles

Most roles in our society are occupied by both men and women. When you refer to people in their roles, avoid references to gender, like the suffix *-man*.

Gender specific	Gender neutral
chairman	chair, chairperson
mailman	mail carrier
male nurse	nurse
policeman	police officer
woman judge	judge
workman	worker

The same rule applies to words that were formerly given the feminine endings *-ess* and *-trix*.

Gender specific	Gender neutral
authoress	author
aviatrix	aviator
poetess	poet
stewardess	flight attendant

Use parallel language to discuss men and women in parallel contexts

Nonparallel	Two students and a coed were accosted at knifepoint.
Parallel	Two male students and a female student were accosted at knifepoint.
Nonparallel	That company hires more men than girls.
Parallel	That company hires more men than women.
Nonparallel	The only guests present are Hank Evans and Mrs. Evans.
Parallel	The only guests present are Hank and Patricia Evans.

b. Weak verbs

Anemic writing results when you connect subjects and complements with linking verbs rather than vigorous verbs. **Linking** (or **copulative**) verbs include *be, become, seem, appear,* and *remain.* Sometimes linking verbs are necessary. But used excessively, they create bland, monotonous prose.

> William LeBaron Jenney *was* the nineteenth-century Chicago architect who *was* the inventor of the skeletal-frame skyscraper.

Occur, take place, prevail, exist, happen, and other verbs expressing a state of affairs can also make your writing colorless.

Weak	In the afternoon a sharp drop in the temperature *occurred.*
Stronger	In the afternoon, the temperature *dropped* sharply.
Weak	Throughout the meeting an atmosphere of increasing tension *existed.*
Stronger	As the meeting progressed, the tension *increased.*

c. Clichés

Much of the time clichés, or stock phrases, are the tritest of metaphors and similes: the *all-American* family, the *land of opportunity,* a *dream come true.* Even a single cliché suggests that you have not bothered to seek out an original way of expressing yourself. Clichés are so insidious in writing precisely because they are so common in speech. Here is a brief sampling:

all boils down to	more than meets the eye
bitter end	other side of the coin
depths of despair	trials and tribulations
heave a sigh of relief	uphill battle
in this day and age	walking on air

Enclosing a cliché in quotation marks does not make it any more acceptable.

d. Mixed figures of speech

Mixed figures of speech result when you stop thinking about the logical and visual sense of what you're writing.

Mixed	I know it sounds like sour grapes, but that's the whole kettle of fish in a nutshell.

e. Empty intensives

Intensives, such as *really, very, so,* and *much,* may emphasize your point in conversation, but they weaken your writing. Instead, try to discover a stronger equivalent of the word in order to convey your precise meaning.

Empty	*Stronger*
really angry	furious, enraged
so happy	joyful, delighted
very bad	detestable, vile

f. Jargon

Professionals often need to use technical language or jargon in professional contexts. What must be eliminated, though, is another kind of jargon: ponderous, wordy, inflated prose that obscures meaning. This is the jargon that most readers object to, the language people use when they hope their inflated prose will raise the commonplace to the significant.

Jargon words are usually abstract rather than concrete, and contain many syllables when a shorter equivalent would be just as (or more) effective. Jargon often contains nouns masquerading as verbs: *finalize, interiorize.* Sometimes jargon consists of nouns turned into adverbs or adjectives by the addition of the suffix *-wise: languagewise, weatherwise, timewise.* Jargon is best deflated by translating it into clear English.

Jargon	The leader-follower relationship must be looked upon as a field situation, and such a field will be structured and sustain its structure only when the views of the leader are acceptable to the followers.
Clearer	A group will fall apart when its members no longer agree with the views of their leader.

g. Pretentious diction

Your diction becomes pretentious if you always choose the polysyllabic word over the shorter one, a Latinate word when an Anglo-Saxon one will do, and flowery phrases in place of simple nouns and verbs.

Pretentious

His vigilant attention to the well-being of others profoundly influences the personal life-styles of all those fortunate enough to bear the appellation of "his friends."

Simpler

His thoughtfulness influences the way his friends live.

Be wary of words that dress up simple facts: *interface* for *meet, utilize* for *use*. Try reading your prose aloud, listening for phrases that seem stilted.

Chapter *13*

Exercise 1 Denotation and Connotation

The following pairs of words have similar denotations but different connotations. Write a sentence using each word in context in order to show clearly the differences.

1. ambulance chaser, victim's advocate

2. domicile, home

3. youthful offender, juvenile delinquent

4. envision, pretend

5. secretive, private

6. deceive, mislead

7. suggest, insinuate

8. surveillance, spying

Chapter 13

Exercise 2 Using Concrete Diction

Write a paragraph about one of the following topics, using abstract, ineffective diction. Then rewrite the paragraph, using more concrete diction.

1. Meals in the campus cafeteria
2. Your backyard
3. A party you recently attended
4. Your brother's or sister's appearance
5. A favorite vacation site

Chapter 13

Exercise 3 Using Idiom Correctly

Underline the correct idiomatic expression in each pair. Consult a dictionary if necessary.

1. The victim's lawyer was impatient (for/with) her trial to begin, since this case differed (from/with) the cases she was accustomed to trying.
2. This was a civil case, in which she aimed (at proving/to prove) that her client had been injured because of a badly constructed fence.
3. The client, a seven-year-old boy named William, was fond (about/of) animals, and he was particularly partial (to/toward) the horses kept in a corral at his uncle's farm.
4. William's uncle frequently had cautioned the boy (against/for) climbing on the rickety boards that formed the corral, but the curious little boy found it hard to comply (to/with) farm rules.
5. Afraid that William would hurt himself on the railing, the uncle replaced the old corral with a metal fence that the manufacturer guaranteed to be superior (than/to) wooden rails.
6. Since the new fence had an electronic gate, William's uncle had the corral inspected by an expert (about/on) electric fences prior (than/to) the boy's visit.
7. After he was assured (of/on) the safety of the metal fence, the uncle instructed William (about/in) the proper operation of the new corral.
8. William, fascinated by the shiny fence, spent an hour opening and closing the electronic mechanism, but he then grew impatient (about/with) how long the gate took to open, and he fell into his old habit of climbing over the railing into the little arena.
9. Unfortunately, as William jumped down, an electrical wire adhered (to/with) his shoe, the fence short-circuited, William received a mild shock and fell into the corral, and the horses stepped on him.
10. Consequently, William developed a fear (about/of) large objects.
11. He confided (in/with) his lawyer that he was especially scared (by/of) horses.
12. The lawyer consulted an authority (about/on) fence design, who said the wiring was faulty.
13. The lawyer was determined that the negligent manufacturer would not profit (by/off) such a badly designed product.
14. She was sure any jury would sympathize (about/with) her client, and she was grateful (about/for) the chance to handle the case.

Chapter 13

Exercise 4 Eliminating Sexist Language

Revise the following sentences to eliminate sexist language without creating awkwardness.

1. Everyone who works in the building must move his car out of the parking lot by noon.

2. I am meeting tomorrow with a woman lawyer to discuss changing my will.

3. "I now pronounce you man and wife," closed the minister.

4. After years of prejudice, in some communities a woman can now become a fireman.

5. Any doctor who wants to be successful needs to be truly dedicated to his patients.

6. Upon first being introduced to the married couple, Mr. Johnson said, "I am so pleased to meet you, Dr. Miller, and you, too, Sarah."

7. Of all the potential congressmen, Amy Potter is the best qualified: she's a sharp, articulate girl.

8. A grade-school teacher can expect her work to be challenging.

9. Each student interested in declaring a major in business should see his adviser this week.

10. As the dance began, the ladies lined up on one side of the room and the men on the other.

11. Being a flight attendant can offer a person the opportunity to visit places she never dreamed of seeing.

12. The paper printed descriptions of the two suspects, a short man of about twenty-five and a tall girl in her thirties.

Chapter 13

Exercise 5 Eliminating Weak Verbs

Underline the weak verbs in the following passage. Then replace them with stronger verbs. You may want to rewrite some of the sentences in order to accommodate your new verbs.

The number of vegetarians in the United States has increased considerably in recent decades, and many institutions are doing things to accommodate this expanding group. For example, airlines now often have vegetarian meals for their passengers. Many restaurants also have a section of their menus with vegetarian entrées. People are vegetarians for many reasons. Many individuals who are concerned about their health do not eat meat because they do not want to get extra cholesterol. Others believe people were not meant to eat meat; they give as proof the vegetarian nature of most primates (baboons being the exception) and the extremely long intestines of human beings. Carnivores, such as cats and dogs, have short intestines, allowing meat to pass through the digestive system quickly. Human intestines are more closely like those of herbivores, such as the horse, whose long intestine slowly gets nutrients from plant food. Vegetarians who hold these ideas also give support for their claims by pointing to the high incidence of colon cancer among meat eaters. Other people do not eat meat for aesthetic reasons; Oscar Wilde, for instance, said he would not eat corpses. Many vegetarians take up the practice because of their strong ethical belief about animal rights. Some of these individuals also do not use leather products and cosmetics or drugs tested on animals. Spiritual beliefs are the motivation for a large percentage of the world's vegetarians: Buddhists, Hindus, and Seventh-Day Adventists. In fact, people of many religious backgrounds do not eat animals because they feel that killing them is morally wrong. Finally, some individuals become vegetarians in recognition that producing meat is an inefficient way to give the world's inhabitants protein; an acre of land used to grow grain can result in several times as much food as an acre of land used to raise cattle.

Chapter 13

Exercise 6 Identifying Mixed Figures of Speech

First, identify the mixed figures of speech by underlining them wherever they appear in the following sentences. Then explain exactly what is wrong with them.

1. The politician claimed to be a team player and promised to take the bull by the horns and clean up the problems of the nation.

2. Freedom is the cornerstone upon which the fabric of our country was built.

3. After years of being a drifter, Timothy finally anchored himself to a steady job and put down roots in Cleveland.

4. The professor's comments failed to illuminate the students, who felt they had stepped into calculus before they were ready; its mysteries remained unfathomable to them.

Chapter 13

Exercise 7 Revising Diction

Revise the following paragraph to eliminate jargon, pretentious diction, empty intensives, and clichés.

In order to maximize the auditory response potentiality for turntable-type stereophonic equipment, several operational guidelines must be adhered to. First, one must utilize a high-fidelity disk that evidences no sign of distress or undue wear. Second, in the eventuality of persistent noise interference or interruption, one should apply a very nonabrasive cleaning cloth to the disk. Next, if there is as yet no acoustic improvement, one should inspect the stylus device for any minute residual atmospheric particles. An excess or a deficit in the gravitational force exerted on the tonearm may be corrected by minor adjustments. Once the mechanism is in operational order, one should minimize the possibility of human error by restraining movements in the immediate vicinity of the mechanism. In the event that there is an absence of all auditory sensation, the operator should inspect the power source for an adequate connection. Soundwise, really true-to-life results will make your day.

Chapter 13

Exercise 8 Revising Diction

Revise the following paragraph to eliminate jargon, pretentious diction, empty intensives, and clichés.

> When you are putting out feelers for a coresident with whom to share your space, you first really need to establish the parameters of acceptable and unacceptable behavior in this interpersonal-type relationship. As you prioritize, consider the advantages of similar life-styles and what you are both into. If you discover that the potential coresident is a music-video junkie while you are looking for meaningful communication with a significant other, then you probably will not relate, roommatewise. Culinary interests should also be quite compatible. Moreover, early birds and night owls do not easily coexist. While you are considering the possibility of coresiding, a few properly considered questions should elicit the desired feedback so that you may avoid a potential blowup situation. If the individual offers only negative input, think twice before you put your John Hancock on that lease.

14   *Sentence Structure*

1. Elements of a Sentence

To analyze grammar, we need to classify the words and groups of words that make up a sentence, to group words that are alike in some respects and to give names to those groups. Although modern linguists have proposed alternative classifications that may well provide a more complete analysis of grammatical structures than the categories of traditional grammar, the traditional classifications have the advantage of simplicity, familiarity, and reasonable consistency. Words in sentences have four functions: to name, to assert, to modify (describe or limit) other words, and to connect other parts of a sentence.

Function	*Class*	*Examples*
to name	substantive	nouns, pronouns, gerunds, infinitives
to assert	predicative	verbs
to describe or limit	modifier	adjectives, adverbs, participles
to join elements	connective	conjunctions, prepositions

Groups of words (or constructions) may have the same function as single words; such groups are called **phrases** or **clauses.**

a. Subject and predicate

The grammatical term for the word or words that name what you are talking about is the **subject.** The **predicate** is the assertion you make about the subject.

Subject	Predicate.
Edison	invented the light bulb.

The subject is usually a noun or a **pronoun** (a word used in place of the noun), although it may be a phrase or a clause. The predicate may contain a number of different words, but the essential part is a **verb.**

b. Modifiers

Modifiers describe nouns and verbs; they may be attached to almost any part of a sentence. Any word that modifies a noun, pronoun, or gerund is an **adjective** in function. An **adverb** is any word that modifies a verb, an adjective, or another adverb. In the following example, *hungry, good,* and *table* are adjectives; *very* is an adverb modifying the adjective *hungry;* and *seldom* is an adverb modifying the verb *display*.

Very hungry people seldom display good table manners.

c. Identifying subject and verb

To analyze any sentence, begin with identifying the simple subject and the verb. First look for the verb, often a word or group of words that states an action. Some forms or tenses of a verb are really phrases, including one or more auxiliary verbs: he *was hit,* he *has been hit,* you *had taken,* you *will have taken*. Some verbs, called **linking verbs,** or **copulas,** merely assert that something is—or looks, sounds, seems, or appears to be—something: He *is* a talented athlete, She *seems* intelligent.

After you have found the verb, put it in the blank in the following question: "Who or what _____?" The answer is the subject, and if you take away the modifiers you have the simple subject: The long, dull *speech* put us all to sleep. In a sentence that asks a question, the subject often follows some form of the very *have* or *be,* or a form of an auxiliary verb.

verb	subject	
Have	you	the time?

auxiliary	subject	verb
Have	you	read this novel?

In an imperative sentence, the subject is not expressed.

subject	verb
( )	Come in.

A sentence may have several nouns as its subjects. Such a construction is called a **compound subject.**

The *trees* and *plants* were blooming.

Similarly, you can make several assertions about one subject. Such a construction is called a **compound predicate.**

She *wrote, revised, typed,* and *proofread* her essay.

d. Complements

Some verbs, called intransitive verbs, require nothing to complete them; in themselves they make a full assertion about the subject.

After meeting all the relatives, my cousin *left*.

Transitive verbs are incomplete by themselves. If you write "I bought," the reader is left hanging and asks, "What did you buy?" The words that complete the assertion are called **complements** of the verb.

I bought *a scarf*.

The most common type of complement is a **direct object,** usually a noun or pronoun but sometimes a phrase or clause. The direct object usually names the thing acted upon by the subject.

subject	verb	direct object
My niece	drew	a *picture*.

The direct object may be compound.

I borrowed a *tent*, a *sleeping bag*, and a *gas stove*.

Certain verbs (usually those involving an act of giving or telling) may take an **indirect object,** a complement that receives whatever is named by the direct object.

The award gave the photographer encouragement.
[What did the award give? *Encouragement* is the direct object. Who received the encouragement? *Photographer* is the indirect object.]

The same meaning can be expressed by a phrase beginning with *to*.

The award gave encouragement *to* the photographer.

Direct and indirect objects are called **object complements. A subject complement,** in contrast, follows a linking verb and completes the predicate by giving another name for the subject or by describing the subject.

My mother was the *major* of the town.

A noun that serves as a subject complement of a linking verb is called a **predicate noun.** Linking verbs may also be completed by an adjective that describes the subject, a **predicate adjective.**

The mayor was *popular*.

e. Phrases

A group of words may have the same function in a sentence as a single word. In the sentence "The train leaves in ten minutes," the group of words *in ten minutes* modifies the verb *leaves* in the same way as an adverb like *soon* would. Such groups of words, which do not make a complete statement but which function like a single word, are **phrases.** They may be named for the kind of word around which they are constructed—prepositional, participial, gerund, or infinitive phrases. They may also be named by the way they function in a sentence—as adjective, adverb, or noun phrases.

Prepositional phrases

A **prepositional phrase** consists of a preposition joined to a noun or a pronoun, which is called the object of the preposition. Such phrases usually modify nouns or verbs, and they are described accordingly as adjective or adverb phrases.

adjective   adverb

The flowers in the yard bloomed in the sun.

Verbals and verb phrases

A **verbal** is a form of verb that functions as some other part of speech. A verbal that modifies a noun is called a **participle.** It may be in the past or the present tense: a *used* [past] car with *splitting* [present] upholstery.

A verb form that functions as a noun is called a **gerund:** *Writing* is his passion. Gerunds may also be used as the objects of verbs or of prepositions: He loves *singing.*

An **infinitive** is a verbal consisting of the present form of the verb preceded by *to: to write, to read.* Infinitives are frequently used as nouns, as subjects or object of the verb: *To err* is human.

Participles, gerunds, and infinitives may take objects, and they may be modified by adverbs or by prepositional phrases. A verbal with its modifier and its object, or subject, makes up a verbal phrase and functions as a single part of speech, but it does not make a full statement.

Participial phrase	*Moved by her speech,* I decided to join the organization.
Gerund phrase	*Selecting an appropriate site* took a lot of time.
Infinitive phrase	The task required us *to walk for hours.*

Absolute phrases

An **absolute phrase** is a group of words that has a subject but no verb and is not grammatically connected to the rest of the sentence. The subject of an absolute phrase is often followed by a participle: *The site having been selected,* we met to choose a sculptor. The subject of an absolute phrase may also be followed by an adjective or a prepositional phrase: She recounted the incident, *her voice angry, her face pale.*

Appositive phrases

An **appositive** is a noun, or noun substitute, added to explain another noun: My mother, *the mayor,* attracted attention all of her life.

f. Clauses

A **clause** is a group of words that contains a subject and a predicate. Every sentence must contain at least one clause.

Independent and dependent clauses

Independent clauses can stand alone as complete sentences. "She heard the news" has a subject and a verb and is a complete sentence. In contrast, some clauses serve only as a subordinate part of the sentence. Called **dependent** (or **subordinate**) **clauses,** they perform a function like that of adjectives, adverbs, or nouns. "When she heard the news" is a clause—it has a subject and verb—but the addition of the word *when* makes the clause dependent. It needs an independent clause added to it to make a complete sentence: When she heard the news, *she was delighted.* Dependent clauses are usually preceded by relative pronouns (*who, which, that*) or by subordinating conjunctions (such as *although, because, if, since, when,* and *while*). Written separately, dependent clauses are sentence fragments. They function like parts of speech.

Noun clauses

A noun clause, which functions as a noun, may be a subject or a complement in a main clause, or the object of a preposition or of a gerund.

That Lauren was considered for the position is remarkable. [subject]

She said *that she would accept* only under certain conditions. [direct object]

We will give the job to *whoever is best qualified.* [object of the preposition]

We do the best for others by asking *what we can do for others.* [object of a gerund]

Adverb clauses

An **adverb clause** is a dependent clause used to modify a verb, adjective, or adverb in the main clause.

We ate *whenever we felt like it.* [modifies the verb]

The trip was as pleasant *as we had hoped.* [modifies the adjective]

The train arrived sooner *than we had expected.* [modifies the adverb]

Adjective clauses and relative pronouns

An **adjective clause** is a dependent clause that modifies a noun or pronoun.

The salesman *we met yesterday* showed us his samples.

Adjective clauses are usually introduced by relative pronouns.

Dorothy Sayers wrote many books *that* were widely read.

2. Sentence Types

a. Simple sentences

A **simple sentence** consists of one independent clause with or without modifiers but with no dependent clause attached to it.

Nervously biting his fingernails, Harvey despaired.

Simple sentences can be quite elaborate.

Harvey and his girlfriend, Zelda, puzzled once more by the red marks on their papers, despaired of ever learning the fine points of grammar.

b. Compound sentences

A **compound sentence** consists of two or more independent clauses joined by a coordinating conjunction (*and, but, for, nor, or, so,* and *yet*) or a semicolon.

Harvey despaired of ever learning the fine points of grammar, but Zelda had hope.

The compound sentence offers you the advantage of balance and antithesis.

c. Complex sentences

A **complex sentence** contains one independent clause and one or more dependent clauses.

> Although Harvey despaired of ever learning the fine points of grammar, Zelda had hope.

You can arrange complex sentences to produce various sentence patterns and to indicate subtle relationships between ideas.

d. Compound-complex sentences

A **compound-complex sentence** contains more than one independent clause and at lease one dependent clause.

Because he had never really studied grammar before, Harvey thought that he would never learn its fine points, but Zelda believed that they would be able to master the subject.

Chapter 14

Exercise 1 Sentence Elements

Underline the simple subjects and the verbs in the following sentences. Note that either the subject or the verb may be compound.

1. Before the advent of railroads, economic activity was largely restricted to areas adjacent to oceans or major rivers.
2. The cost of overland transportation was many times that of ship and barge.
3. The large commercial centers and important cities of the world were located near large bodies of water.
4. Only for the most expensive luxury goods could the cost of overland transport be justified.
5. The railroad provided the first economical method of moving large quantities of goods overland and thereby greatly affected commerce.
6. Areas like the Great Plains of the United States could not have been settled without the railroad.
7. Without a wide network of navigable rivers, transporting the agricultural products raised in the Great Plains would have been almost impossible.
8. Despite incredible technological advances such as air travel, railroads continue to be an important means not only of moving people from place to place but also of promoting commerce.

Chapter 14

Exercise 2 Sentence Elements

Underline and label the subjects (S) and verbs (V) in the following sentences. Label direct objects (DO), indirect objects (IO), predicate nouns (PN), and predicate adjectives (PA).

1. The art of acupuncture first was mentioned in Chinese writings in about the twenty-eighth century B.C.

2. According to the theory, there are more than eight hundred special points on the human body; they are linked to organs.

3. Good health involves the flow of energy through these acupuncture points, and the two energies, yin and yang, must be balanced.

4. Inserting needles into different points directs the flow properly, restoring health.

5. Although thorns and sticks often were used in ancient times, needles now are made of copper, silver, and gold.

6. Certain materials are best for specific ailments.

7. To detect illness early, an acupuncturist practices a method of diagnosis involving pulse points.

8. Acupuncture first was used in the West in the mid-twentieth century, but much of the medical community remains skeptical.

9. Other doctors, however, have incorporated the technique into their practice.

10. The method is popular as an anesthetic, and it may have even broader uses.

11. For example, in 1977 a clinic opened in Hong Kong for the acupuncture treatment of drug addicts.

12. Acupuncture sometimes has taken the form of staplepuncture; in this procedure a staple inserted into the earlobe supposedly reduces dependency on drugs, alcohol, or nicotine.

13. Are such desperate people simply ready to give up their habits?

14. Regardless, acupuncture may offer some patients an alternative to drugs or surgery.

Chapter 14

Exercise 3 Phrases

Underline the phrases in the following sentences. Label them as prepositional (prep), participial (part), gerund (ger), infinitive (inf), or appositive (app).

1. Developing along with industrialization, advertising became a big business in America in the mid-nineteenth century.

2. Between the early years of advertising and today, the techniques and function of the business have changed.

3. Now the goal of advertising is often creating a market.

4. The average American, exposed to as many as a thousand ads every day, is affected in many ways by their messages.

5. For example, to hear someone hum a soft-drink jingle is not unusual.

6. Two popular books, *The Hidden Persuaders* and *Subliminal Seduction,* discuss the sometimes subtle manipulation that ads can accomplish.

7. Revealing little real information, many advertisements sell an image.

8. Portraying stereotypical images of African-Americans and women was for many years standard practice.

9. Changes recently having been made, ads may still place additional demands on already-pressured people.

10. A woman may now be featured as a professional during the day, but she is then expected to go home, to feed the children, and, with perfect makeup, to greet her husband with a smile.

11. Men in ads, modeled on athletes and movie stars, often convey the message that every adult male must be simultaneously rugged, successful, and sensitive.

12. Fortunately, to enjoy an ad we need not accept its values.

Chapter 14

Exercise 4 Clauses

In each sentence, put brackets around the dependent clauses, if any. Then label the simple subject (S) and verb (V) of all clauses, dependent and main.

1. In recent decades, people have become increasingly aware of the problem of wildlife extinction, which affects almost every part of the world.

2. Extinction, of course, is not a new phenomenon; dinosaurs disappeared without any help from human beings.

3. However, many species have suffered extinction or are endangered because people have not behaved responsibly.

4. Some animals are threatened by hunters who kill not an occasional animal for their own use but thousands of animals that will be used for luxury items, such as furs or ivory.

5. The African elephant has been wiped out in many locales, and certain whales that once filled the oceans are now almost completely gone.

6. Most of the danger to animals has come from human thoughtlessness or greed, often in the name of progress, resulting in the destruction of many animals' natural habitats.

7. In all of its forms, pollution poses another threat to many kinds of wildlife that inhabit both rural and urban areas.

8. Despite our growing consciousness and regrets, animals that are already extinct cannot be brought back.

9. Living ones, however, can be protected, and conservation efforts are beginning to yield results.

10. Restrictions on trade and bans on hunting and whaling protect endangered species and allow them time to increase their population.

11. To further the cause of preservation, educational and fund-raising projects are supported by such groups as Greenpeace, the Sierra Club, and the World Wildlife Fund.

12. National parks and refuges throughout the world, while ensuring that the natural habitats of wildlife are preserved, also provide places of recreation and retreat for human beings.

13. More and more people are beginning to realize that the welfare of the earth's wildlife, far from being an overly idealistic concern, is our welfare.

Chapter *14*

Exercise 5 Sentence Types

Classify the following sentences as simple (S), compound (CD), complex (CX), or compound-complex (CC).

1. Mardi Gras, which means "Fat Tuesday," is the last day of feasting and festivity before the forty days of Lent. _____

2. In nineteenth-century Paris, the celebration took the form of a Roman sacrificial procession: a fattened ox led through the city. _____

3. Some people returning from Paris in 1827 organized New Orleans's first Mardi Gras parade, but the celebration did not become an annual event until thirty years later. _____

4. Although Mardi Gras is celebrated in a number of places in the world, in the United States nothing can compare to the citywide party that New Orleans hosts. _____

5. Each year, organizations called *krewes* begin planning the festivities months before the Mardi Gras season. _____

6. The *krewes* plan the formal ball that will be held for members, design elaborate floats, and order "throws." _____

7. Throws are trinkets of various sorts that the *krewe* members toss from the floats to the crowd; beads and doubloons are the most common throws, but *krewes* also throw such novelty items as cups, umbrellas, and even giant toothbrushes. _____

8. Although Mardi Gras itself is Shrove Tuesday, the parades begin several weeks earlier. _____

9. A giant free party, the celebration draws thousands of tourists to the city. _____

10. On Mardi Gras, the parade routes are overflowing with local people and visitors, who have in common their desire to enjoy themselves. _____

11. Standing out in the crowds are people dressed like clowns, movie characters, and giant crawfish, among many other things. _____

12. In the French Quarter, which is even more crowded, people become particularly uninhibited. _____

13. Despite the number of people, Mardi Gras is remarkably safe, although you may be in danger of getting your hand stepped on as you reach for beads or a doubloon on the ground. _____

14. Even the most reserved, calm people may be transformed by the Mardi Gras spirit. _____

15. By nine o'clock that night, the last float has passed and the last sounds of jazz are starting to fade, but the preparations that are so important to this event will begin all over again in only weeks. _____

Chapter

15   *Agreement*

Most nouns and all verbs have different singular and plural forms. For a sentence to make grammatical sense, use singular verbs with singular subjects, and plural verbs with plural subjects. Pronouns, too, have separate forms to indicate number (singular or plural) and person (first person: *I, we;* second person: *you;* third person: *he, she, it, they*). The matching of subjects and verbs, pronouns and nouns, according to person and number in a sentence is called **agreement.**

1. Agreement of Subject and Verb

In general, plural nouns and singular verbs in the third-person singular present usually end in *-s,* whereas singular nouns and plural verbs usually do not:

Singular (verb ends in *-s*)	The clock ticks loudly.
	The star shines faintly.
Plural (noun ends in *-s*)	The clocks tick loudly.
	The stars shine faintly.

This rule holds most of the time, but English includes some nouns whose singular and plural forms end in *-s,* as well as a few irregular nouns whose plural forms do not end in *-s* (*man, woman, child, tooth, sheep*). These unusual forms do not affect the correct form of the verb.

Singular (some nouns end in *-s*)	That bus looks unreliable.
	Gas sells for less.
Plural (some irregular nouns do not end in *-s*)	Her feet feel tired.
	Those phenomena are inexplicable

These are the basic rules for subject-verb agreement in English. But several grammatical situations are sometimes confusing, cases in which at first you may not see how to apply those rules.

a. Modifying phrases after the subject

A modifying phrase placed between the subject and verb may seem to change the number of the subject, but it does not.

Incorrect	A program of two Bergman films *were shown* last night.
Correct	A program of two Bergman films *was shown* last night.

Although phrases such as *accompanied by, as well as,* and *together with* suggest a plural idea, they do not change the number of the subject.

Incorrect	The prisoner, accompanied by guards and her lawyer, *were* in the courtroom.
Correct	The prisoner, accompanied by guards and her lawyer, *was* in the courtroom.

b. Compound subject

When two subjects are joined by *and,* they are usually considered to be plural.

Science and math *are* my best subjects.

When two nouns are used together to indicate a single idea, use a singular verb.

Bacon and eggs *is* a typical American breakfast.

Similarly, when the two nouns of a compound subject both refer to the same person or thing, use a singular verb.

The young bachelor and man-about-town *was* finally discovered to be an impostor.

When *each* or *every* modifies a compound subject, use a singular form of the verb.

Every camera and light meter *has* been reduced in price.

c. Collective nouns

Collective nouns, such as *class, committee, team, family,* and *number,* are treated as singular when they refer to the group as a unit. If you want to emphasize the individual members of the group, you may use the plural form of the verb.

The committee *was* unanimous in its recommendations.

The committee *were* divided in their recommendations.

The number of correct answers *was* small.

A number of papers *are* overdue. [*Number* is singular when preceded by *the,* plural when preceded by *a.*]

d. Nouns ending in -*s*

Some nouns that are plural in form are grammatically singular, such as *aesthetics, economics, linguistics, mathematics, news, physics,* and *semantics.*

Physics *was* the hardest course I took in high school.

Certain other nouns ending in -*s* have no singular form and are always plural—for example, *trousers, scissors, measles, forceps.* Finally, some nouns ending in -*ics*—such as *athletics, politics,* and *statistics*—may be either singular or plural, often with a distinction in meaning.

Athletics [the collective activity] *builds* the physique.

Athletics [particular activities] *are* her favorite pastime.

e. Linking verbs

When two nouns in a sentence are connected by some form of the verb *be,* the first of the nouns is the subject; the verb always agrees with it.

Incorrect	The first thing visible on the horizon were the tuna boats.
Correct	The first thing visible on the horizon was the tuna boats.
Correct	The tuna boats were the first thing visible on the horizon.

f. Inverted sentence order

When the subject of a sentence follows the verb, the subject and verb must still agree.

| Incorrect | Beyond the old fort was the endless sands of the desert. |

Correct	Beyond the old fort were the endless sands of the desert.

In sentences beginning with *there is* or *there are, there* is called an expletive and is not the subject. In these cases, the real subject of the sentence always follows the verb.

There *is* only one *solution* to this problem.

There *are* three possible *solutions* to this problem.

g. *Or/nor*

When two subjects are joined by *or* or *nor,* the verb agrees with the subject nearer it.

Neither Sam nor his *sisters have* ever been abroad.

Neither his sisters nor *Sam has* ever been abroad.

h. Indefinite pronouns

Some indefinite pronouns are always singular: *anybody, anyone, each, either, everybody, everyone, neither, nobody, no one, one, somebody, someone.* They are always followed by singular verb forms.

Anyone not admitted *is* guaranteed a refund.

Each of the students *was* tested.

Other indefinite pronouns may be singular or plural: *all, any, more, most, none, some.* To determine whether the pronoun is singular or plural, look at the noun that it refers to.

None of the money *was* lost.

None of the coins *were* lost.

A few indefinite pronouns are always plural: *both, few, fewer, many, others, several.*

Others are still waiting to apply, even though *fewer* than half *are* likely to be interviewed.

i. Relative pronouns as subjects

The relative pronouns *who, which,* and *that,* when used as subjects of subordinate clauses, take a singular verb when their antecedent in the sentence is singular and a plural verb when it is plural.

The school was destroyed by high *winds,* which *are* unusual at this time of year.

The correct number of the relative pronoun may be harder to determine when the sentence contains the phrase *one of the* or *one of those.*

This is one of those inexpensive *watches* that *are* so popular today. [*That* refers to the group of watches.]

I selected the only *one* of the watches that *is* guaranteed. [*That* refers to just one of the watches.]

2. Agreement of Pronoun and Antecedent

Pronouns agree in number with their antecedents, the words in a sentence they refer to.

Many *people* pay a genealogist to trace *their* ancestry.

Like subject-verb agreement, a few unusual constructions may at first seem confusing.

a. Compound antecedents

Compound antecedents are usually considered plural when joined by *and* and singular when joined by *or* or *nor.*

My father encouraged Henry and David to postpone *their* trip.

Neither the *dog* nor the *cat* had touched *its* food.

b. Collective nouns as antecedents

When the antecedent is a collective noun, use the singular pronoun to emphasize the cohesiveness of the group, the plural to emphasize separate individuals.

The team *was* undefeated in *its* first season.

The team *were* varied in *their* abilities.

c. Indefinite antecedents

In informal usage, indefinite pronouns—*anybody, anyone, each, either, everybody, everyone, neither, nobody, no one, somebody, someone*—are often treated as if they were plural.

Informal	Almost *everyone* eats fruit as part of *their* diet.

However, all of these pronouns are singular, and pronouns that follow them in Edited English must also be singular. Unfortunately, English lacks singular personal pronouns that can refer to both males and females. Consequently, sentences such as the following, while grammatically correct, exclude half of the human population:

Anyone returning merchandise must present *his* sales receipt.

No one in line got *her* money back.

One solution to this problem is to use two pronouns when the antecedent can be either male or female.

No one in line got *his or her* money back.

While at times this solution is effective, at other times it results in awkwardness.

For once, *everyone* in the class saw *himself or herself* as *he or she* really was.

Another correct—and less awkward—solution is to simply rewrite the sentence with plural nouns and pronouns.

For once, *members* of the class saw *themselves* as they really were.

Similar agreement problems may also arise when the antecedent is a singular noun that is not intended to refer to a specific person, place, or thing.

Incorrect	If a customer isn't satisfied with their purchase, we will refund their money.

Correct this agreement error by using either singular forms for both the pronoun and its antecedent or plural forms for both.

Correct	If customers aren't satisfied with their purchases, we will refund their money.

d. Demonstrative pronouns

When you use demonstrative pronouns—*this, that, these, those*—as adjectives, they must agree in number with the words they modify. Use *this* and *that* with singular nouns, *these* and *those* with plural nouns.

Incorrect	These kind of vegetables are grown here.
Correct	This kind of vegetable is grown here.
Correct	These kinds of vegetables are grown here.

Chapter 15

Exercise 1 Subject-Verb Agreement

Underline the correct verb in the following sentences.

1. Every one of the nine men on the team (is, are) important.
2. The close relationship with professors and fellow students (makes, make) the small college the choice of many entering freshmen.
3. Doug sprawled in the chair and knocked over one of the lamps which (was, were) on display.
4. There (has, have) never been hard feelings between the two neighbors.
5. The symptoms of lead poisoning (varies, vary) with each case.
6. Next in the waiting line (was, were) an elderly woman and her grandson.
7. The principal believes that athletics (improves, improve) school morale.
8. Up goes the starter's gun, and each of the runners (becomes, become) tense.
9. The doctor said that there is always a possibility that the infection will return but that so far there (has, have) been no signs of its recurrence.
10. The family (takes, take) its annual vacation during August.
11. Each of the hospital's patients (has, have) some kind of medical insurance.
12. Either the *Times* or the *Tribune* (is, are) a reliable source of news.
13. The catcher, as well as the pitcher and coach, (was, were) arguing furiously with the umpire.
14. Her chief interest in life (was, were) politics.
15. Slater is one of those legislators who (has, have) always opposed spending.

Chapter 15

Exercise 2 Subject-Verb Agreement

In the following sentences, underline and correct the errors, if any, in subject-verb agreement.

1. Parents whose children are grown or an adult who has no contact with children is probably unaware of what a large market there is in children's toys.
2. The price tag on many toys is startling, often out of the range of the mother or father who want to buy them.
3. The purchase of expensive toys also create the negative effect of pointing out to children the economic differences between other youngsters and themselves.
4. The concept behind many contemporary toys seem to reflect little imagination.
5. Often born of television, each of these new toys come with ready-made names and histories.
6. Also important is changes in how parents choose toys for boys and girls.
7. An increasing sensitivity to sex stereotypes have resulted in an awareness that children's toys have consequences that extends beyond playtime.
8. If parents have two children, there exists no reasons that the girl shouldn't play with dolls and the boy with a chemistry set.
9. The problem of stereotyping arises when a boy or girl are not allowed the opportunity to experiment with contrasting toys and roles.
10. Sometimes, everyone in the family except the children play with the new, fancy toys.
11. Finally, though, the child, not the adults, are who counts in the eyes of manufacturers.
12. A marketing team knows that it is the children who make or break a toy—usually the latter.

Chapter 15

Exercise 3 Agreement

In the following sentences, underline and correct the errors, if any, in subject-verb agreement and pronoun agreement.

1. A twentieth-century man or woman probably think of greed when they hear of alchemy, the attempt to turn base metals into gold.
2. Actually, a major issue alchemists were concerned with were larger philosophical views about the relationship between human beings and nature.
3. References to alchemy appears in the eighth century B.C. in China and India.
4. In the Western world, discussions and explanations of alchemy dates at least from twelfth-century texts written in Latin.
5. Apparently, each of the many alchemists in these different cultures were searching for a way to prolong life and understand the creator.
6. Mysticism, ritual, and secrecy surrounds the subject in the books passed down to modern scholars.
7. Perhaps more important now, the elements of early science were discovered through alchemy.
8. In the sixteenth and seventeenth centuries, work in alchemy paralleled the scientific revolution, and the mystical connotations and spiritual purpose was lost.
9. Especially important were the alchemists' emphasis on close observation and on careful empirical studies.
10. In the course of these kind of alchemical experiment, mineral acids and alcohol was discovered, and the process of distilling liquids was developed.
11. As science progressed, however, interest in the practice waned, and the scientific community expressed their contempt by labeling alchemists quacks.
12. Had anyone really known how to turn metal into gold, they probably would have preserved the technique.
13. However, there is in existence no accounts of the practice that provide evidence of success.
14. Neither alchemists nor the modern scientist seem capable of such a feat.

Chapter

16

Case of Pronouns and Nouns

Case refers to the changes in form of a noun or pronoun that show how it is used in a sentence. The only case forms for nouns in modern English are those that indicate possession (*child's, woman's*). Most pronouns, however, have three case forms: the nominative (or subjective) case, when the pronoun is the subject of a verb; the possessive (or genitive) case, to show possession; and the objective case, when the pronoun functions as the object of a verb or preposition.

Nominative:	I	you	he/she/it	we	they	who
Possessive:	my	your	his/her/its	our	their	whose
Objective:	me	you	him/her/it	us	them	whom

Usually you will use the right case without having to think about it. But because incorrect pronoun case is so often heard in informal speech, you should not always trust your ears to guide you correctly.

1. Compound Constructions

A noun and pronoun used together in a compound construction should be in the same case. In most of these situations, you can determine whether you have the pronoun in the right case by reading the sentence without the noun. The sentence should still sound correct.

Incorrect	The doctor asked *my mother* and *I* to come in.
Correct	The doctor asked *my mother* and *me* to come in. [objective case]
Incorrect	My brother and *me* went to the movies.
Correct	My brother and *I* went to the movies. [nominative case]
Incorrect	Our parents always rewarded *we children* for getting good grades.

Correct	Our parents always rewarded *us children* for getting good grades. [objective case]
Incorrect	The float was designed by only two members of the class, Howard and *I*.
Correct	The float was designed by only two members of the class, Howard and *me*. [objective case]
Incorrect	Between you and *I*, this essay hasn't got a chance of winning the contest.
Correct	Between you and *me*, this essay hasn't got a chance of winning the contest. [objective case]

2. *Who* and *Whom* in Dependent Clauses

When in doubt about the case of the relative pronoun *who* or *whoever*, try a personal pronoun (*he/him, she/her, they/them*) in its place in the sentence. If *he, she,* or *they* sounds right, use the nominative, *who*. If *him, her,* or *them* fits, use the objective, *whom*.

Here is the woman *who*/whom can explain eclipses.
[We can't say "*her* can explain eclipses." "*She* can explain eclipses" is correct, so use *who*.]

Marshall is the man who/*whom* I told you about.
[The clause means "I told you about *him*," so the correct pronoun is *whom*.]

Note that the case of the pronoun *who* or *whom* is unaffected by the insertion of phrases like *I think* or *we know* into the dependent clause.

The artist *who*/whom I thought would design the awards has changed her mind.
[The clause means "I thought that *she* would design the awards." *Who* is correct.]

3. *Who* and *Whom* in Interrogatives

To determine the correct case of the interrogative pronouns *who* and *whom*, apply the same test described for dependent clauses. If the answer to the question includes the nominative form of the personal pronoun, *who* is the correct interrogative; if the answer includes the objective form, *whom* is correct.

Who is coming to the party? [*They* are coming.]

Whom are you expecting to come to the party? [I am expecting *them*.]

In speech and in much informal writing, the tendency is to use *who*, no matter what its grammatical place in the sentence. Edited English requires that you observe the distinction between *who* and *whom*.

4. Reflexive and Intensive Pronouns

Use reflexive pronouns to refer to a noun or pronoun mentioned earlier in a sentence.

Nominative form	*Reflexive form*
I, we	myself, ourselves
you	yourself, yourselves
he/she/it, they	himself/herself/itself, themselves

Note that the following forms do not exist except in nonstandard usage: *hisself, themself, theirselves.*

Use the reflexive form of the pronoun instead of the objective form whenever the actor in a sentence and the recipient of the action are the same.

Scott accidentally cut *himself.*

We had never seen *ourselves* on television before.

You may use a reflexive pronoun *only* if the noun or pronoun to which it refers also appears in the sentence.

Incorrect	Gina and *myself* are leaving soon.
Correct	Gina and *I* are leaving soon.
Incorrect	He gave the invitation to my sister and *myself.*
Correct	He gave the invitation to my sister and *me.*

When these pronoun forms are used to emphasize a noun or another pronoun in a sentence, rather than to designate the recipient of an action, they are called *intensive pronouns*.

Scott himself was responsible for the accident.

5. Pronouns after *than, as,* and *but*

After *than* or *as,* the case of a pronoun is determined by its use in the shortened clause of which it is a part.

My cousin is taller than *I* [am].

I can type as well as *he* [can].

Sometimes a comparison involving *than* or *as* can be completed in two possible ways. The case of the pronoun will determine how the reader understands the sentence.

They like Kelly more than *I* [do].

They like Kelly more than [they like] me.

The word *but* is sometimes used as a preposition meaning "*except.*" In such constructions, the object of *but* should be in the objective case.

By midnight everyone had left but *them*.

6. Pronouns as Complements of the Verb

In formal writing, the complement of the linking verb *be* is in the nominative case.

Incorrect	It appears that the members of the delegation will be Mr. Rosen, Ms. Kowalski, and *me*.
Correct	It appears that the members of the delegation will be Mr. Rosen, Ms. Kowalski, and *I*.

However, when the complement follows the infinitive form *to be,* use the objective case.

I wouldn't want *to be him*.

7. Pronouns with Infinitives

Use the objective case for both the subject and the object of an infinitive (usually a verb form preceded by *to*).

Subject of infinitive	The company president wanted *me to lie* when I testified before the committee.
Object of infinitive	I would not like *to be him* when the wrongdoing is revealed.

8. Pronouns and Nouns with Gerunds

Gerunds function in a sentence like nouns. Therefore, a noun or pronoun modifying a gerund must be in the possessive case.

Incorrect	Alan's parents disapproved of *him traveling* alone in Greece.
Correct	Alan's parents disapproved of *his traveling* alone in Greece.
Incorrect	They also objected to his *sister bicycling* through Canada.
Correct	They also objected to his *sister's bicycling* through Canada.

Chapter 16

Exercise 1 Pronoun Case

Underline the correct pronoun case forms in the following sentences.

1. My sister is a better skier than (I/me).
2. Had Harvey not found such a good job, his parents never would have accepted such an extravagant gift from his wife and (he/him).
3. There was no comment from the two members (who/whom) I thought were sure to protest.
4. All the students (who/whom) I talked to seemed to like the new coach.
5. My father used to complain to us—my sister and (I/me)—about our using his razor to shave our legs.
6. All the class went on the field trip but (I/me).
7. The new dictator won't be sure of (who/whom) he can trust.
8. His mother is annoyed by (him/his) watching sports every spare minute.
9. The reward was divided between my friend and (I/me).
10. The neighbors have not lived here as long as (ourselves/us/we).
11. Last year we finally had a teacher (who/whom) won the respect of all of (us/we) students (who/whom) were in her class.
12. Only two members of my family are not tone-deaf, my mother and (I/me/ myself).
13. Another good reason for (him/his) joining the Coast Guard is the chance for special training.
14. The ten remaining tickets will be given to (whoever/whomever) applies first.
15. I would hate to be (he/him).

Chapter 16

Exercise 2 Case

Underline the correct case forms in the following sentences.

1. Last year my brother, Bob, decided to marry the woman (who/whom) he had been dating for three years, Cathy.
2. My sister and (I/me/myself) thought it was about time, but one member of the family (who/whom) I thought would be pleased was not as happy as (us/we).
3. Apparently, my grandfather objects to (Bob/Bob's) marrying someone (who/whom) has been divorced.
4. He insisted that he would never approve of a marriage between Bob and (her/she).
5. We knew that Granddad is a man (who/whom) has strong, if old-fashioned, principles; it is true that he does not ask of my siblings and (I/me) more than he expects of (himself/hisself).
6. (Us/We) grandchildren—my brother, my sister, and (I/me/myself)—decided we needed to sit down and talk about the problem.
7. No one loves my grandfather more than (I/me), but I argued that my brother needed to be firm with him.
8. As sad as it made my brother, he agreed that if the choice were between Cathy and Granddad, no one was more important than (her/she).
9. Despite the consensus between my sister and (I/me) that Bob had made the right decision about Granddad, we still felt terrible that two people would be missing from the wedding—my grandma and (he/him).
10. On the day of the wedding, we were happy about everything but (he/him).
11. However, to my surprise, this man (who/whom) I thought would never relent was the first one at the church.
12. When I arrived, there in the very front row sat my grandma and (he/him), after all.
13. Just between you and (I/me), I have a feeling that Granddad knew all along that there was no doubt about (him/his) attending the wedding of his only grandson.

17 *Adjectives and Adverbs*

Adjectives modify nouns or pronouns; they provide such information as the color, size, or manner of the words they describe.

The car came to a *sudden* stop.

Adverbs modify verbs, adjectives, or other adverbs. They answer questions like *When? Where? Why? In what way? To what degree?*

The car *suddenly* stopped.

Most adverbs are formed by adding *-ly* to the adjective: *clear, clearly.* But some adjectives and adverbs have the same form, and a few have completely different forms. Finally, some adjectives already end in *-ly.* A dictionary is your best guide.

1. Comparative and Superlative Forms

a. Of adjectives

Adjectives usually form the comparative by adding *-er* and the superlative by adding *-est.*

lively	livelier	liveliest

Many adjectives of two syllables and all longer adjectives form the comparative and superlative by adding *more* and *most.*

ambitious	more ambitious	most ambitious

All adjectives indicate lesser degree by adding *less* for the comparative and *least* for the superlative.

lively	less lively	least lively

b. Of adverbs

Adverbs nearly always form the comparative with *more* and the superlative with *most.*

slowly	more slowly	most slowly

A few adverbs that do not end in -*ly* form the comparative by adding -*er* and the superlative by adding -*est*.

> fast   faster   fastest

All adverbs indicate lesser degree by adding *less* for the comparative and *least* for the superlative.

> slowly   less slowly   least slowly

c. Irregular comparative and superlative forms

Irregular adjectives

bad	worse	worst
good	better	best
little	less	least
many	more	most
much	more	most
some	more	most

Irregular adverbs

badly	worse	worst
well	better	best

d. Adjectives and adverbs without comparative and superlative forms

Some adjectives and adverbs, like *unique/uniquely, perfect/perfectly, infinite/infinitely,* and *chief/chiefly,* cannot logically take comparative or superlative forms. If necessary, you may use modifiers like *nearly* and *almost* that indicate an approach to the absolute.

e. Correct use of comparative and superlative forms

Use the comparative form for comparisons involving two items, and the superlative for three or more.

> Of my *two* brothers, Jack is the *taller*.

> Of *all* my many relatives, Jack is the *tallest*.

Be careful to avoid double comparisons, constructions that combine *more* or *most, less* or *least* with an adjective or adverb that already ends in *-er* or *-est*.

| Incorrect | I prefer this *more darker* shade of green. |
| Correct | I prefer this *darker* shade of green. |

2. Adjectives with Linking Verbs

Linking verbs such as *be, become, seem,* and *appear,* as well as verbs associated with the senses (*look, feel, taste, sound, smell*) and certain other verbs suggesting development (*become, grow, prove*), are often used to link a subject and a modifying adjective, the subject complement.

| The swimmer | was seemed looked felt became | cold. |

A subject complement can never be an adverb.

| Incorrect | I felt *badly* about her accident. |
| Correct | I felt *bad* about her accident. |

A verb in the list above may be followed by an adverb, but in such an instance it ceases to function as a linking verb.

Adjective and linking verb	Gail looked *tired* to me. [I thought she appeared to be tired.]
Adverb	Gail looked *tiredly* to me. [She turned to me in a tired manner.]
Adjective and linking verb	My opponent's argument proved *convincing*. [It was a convincing argument.]
Adverb	My opponent's argument proved *convincingly* that she had prepared for the debate. [It offered convincing proof that she was prepared.]

3. Nouns Used as Adjectives

Many things and concepts are identified by noun-plus-noun combinations: *light bulb, sofa bed, gas station, computer literacy*. When you use nouns as adjectives, more than three nouns in a row can create a dense, confusing sentence.

Confusing	The *spring office softball tournament preparations* are proceeding smoothly.
Clearer	Preparations for the office's spring softball tournament are proceeding smoothly.

4. Compound Adjectives

When a compound adjective is formed from two nouns, from an adjective and a noun, or from two adjectives, hyphenate the compound when it precedes the noun that it modifies.

The *locker-room* brawl left six players injured.

This book is also available in a *large-print* edition.

Hyphenate all the elements of a phrase used as an adjective.

Peter knew the invitation was a *once-in-a-lifetime* opportunity.

Remember that *-ly* adverbs used with adjectives are modifiers, not part of a compound. Do not hyphenate them.

Their first apartment was in an *exceptionally decrepit* building.

However, similar constructions with *well* usually are hyphenated when they precede the modified noun: a *well-done* steak (but a steak *well done*).

5. Colloquial Forms

In some spoken contexts, these pairs of modifiers are used interchangeably: *real/really, sure/surely, almost/most*. Note that written English demands careful distinctions between them.

Real is an adjective; *really* (meaning "truly") is an adverb.

Acceptable in some speech	Lately, Steve hasn't been sleeping *real* well.

| Preferred in writing | Lately, Steve hasn't been sleeping *really* well. |

Sure is an adjective; *surely* is an adverb.

| Acceptable in some speech | Steve *sure* looks tired in the morning. |
| Preferred in writing | Steve *surely* looks tired in the morning. |

When *most* functions as an adverb, it means "very" or "to the greatest extent." Do not use it in writing to mean "nearly," a sense reserved for the adverb *almost*.

| Acceptable in some speech | *Most* every night he paces the floor. |
| Preferred in writing | *Almost* every night he paces the floor. |

Chapter *17*

Exercise 1 Adjectives and Adverbs

Correct the use of adjectives and adverbs in the following sentences so that it conforms to the standards of formal written English.

That the left and right hemispheres of the brain have very unique functions was realized in the nineteenth century. Physicians noticed that a tumor on one side of the brain most always affects the opposite side of the body; the left hemisphere controls the right side of the body and the right controls the left side. Damage to either side impairs functioning in real different ways. Early research included split-brain surgery, an operation in which the tissue connecting the two hemispheres was separated fully. The effects of complete severing the hemispheres are apparent in a classic example. If you give a split-brain patient a familiar object in her right hand without letting her see the object, she will name it accurate. If you then put the object in her left hand, even if she is able to feel it good, she will become real confused and will not be able to say what it is, because the right hemisphere is nonverbal. The right side also appears to be more spatially oriented and intuitiver than the left, and damage to the right badly impairs a person's ability to recognize faces. The left side, believed to be the most rational, seems analytical and verbal. Some people find this dichotomy interesting because it corresponds good to stereotypes about men and women. Other researchers have even tentative speculated that our dual brain accounts for our tendency to think in dichotomies. Hemisphere specialization develops slow as a person matures; an infant can usually adapt easily to hemisphere damage, but later, after specialization, the effects of damage are more profounder. If this topic provides fertile ground for researchers, it is perhaps even profitabler for the writers of self-help books purporting to teach people how to develop the most full potential of both sides of their brains.

18 *Verbs*

1. Verb Forms

Verbs not only present an action or condition, but also indicate a time frame within which the action or condition occurs—at present, in the past, or in the future. This indication of time depends on verb forms known as tenses. The first of these forms—base, past, and past participle—are the principle parts of a verb. Verbs are classified as regular or irregular.

	Regular verbs	Irregular verbs	
Base	trust	sing	have
Past	trusted	sang	had
Past participle	trusted	sung	had
Present participle	trusting	singing	having
-s form	trusts	sings	has

Irregular verbs form their principles in unpredictable ways. One irregular verb, *be*, is exceptional in that it has eight different forms instead of five:

Base	be
Past	was, were
Past participle	been
Present participle	being
-s form	is
Additional forms	am, are

2. Irregular Verbs

Below are a few of the most common irregular verbs. Your dictionary is a more complete guide.

Base	Past	Past participle
arise	arose	arisen
awake	awoke/awaked	awaked/awoken
choose	chose	chosen
drink	drank	drunk
eat	ate	eaten

fling	flung	flung
lay (put)	laid	laid
lie (recline)	lay	lain
ring	rang	rung
write	wrote	written

The following *regular* verbs are sometimes confused with irregular verbs:

dive/dived/dived
[Avoid *dove,* a regional variation.]
hang/hanged/hanged
In the sense "to execute," *hang* is a regular verb.
lie/lied/lied
In the sense "to tell an untruth," *lie* is a regular verb.
weave/weaved/weaved
In the sense "to move in and out," *weave* is a regular verb.

3. Verb Tenses

a. Present tense

The present tense designates a current act or condition, or an act that is regularly repeated.

Some scientists *believe* that the greenhouse effect *is* already apparent.

The present tense is also used in discussions of literary or artistic works.

When Hamlet *is* alone, he *contemplates* suicide.

Combined with modifiers that indicate time, the present tense can assert that an act or condition will occur in the future.

My flight *leaves* at eight o'clock.

b. Past tense

The past tense designates an act or condition that occurred at a specific time in the past.

On September 7, 1940, the German Luftwaffe *began* its night bombing of London.

The past tense also indicates recurrent actions in the past that have not continued into the present.

Every night for two months, Londoners *took* refuge from the bombs in the city's vast network of subway stations.

c. Future tense

The future tense designates an act or condition that will occur in the future. It is formed by preceding the base form of the verb with *will* or *shall*. (The differences between *will* and *shall* have largely disappeared.)

The doctor *will see* you first thing in the morning.

d. Present perfect tense

The present perfect tense designates an act or condition that occurred at an indefinite time in the past, or one that began in the past and continues into the present. It is formed by preceding the participle form of the verb with *have* or *has*.

Professor Berz has finished her most recent novel.

e. Past perfect tense

The past perfect tense designates an act completed or a condition existing in the past before some specific time in the past. It is formed by preceding the past participle form of the verb with *had*.

I *had* already *composed* my letter of resignation when the telephone rang.

f. Future perfect tense

The future perfect tense designates an act that will be completed or a condition that will exist before some specific time in the future. It is formed by preceding the past participle form of the verb with *will have*.

By March 1, the state transportation department *will have submitted* its plans for the new highway to the airport.

g. Progressive forms

Each of the verb tenses in English also has a progressive form to indicate that an act extends continuously over a period of time. The progressive form is created by substituting the present participle for the form of the verb used in each tense and adding a form of the verb *be*. Compare each of the following sentences with their counterparts above.

Present progressive	The earth's average temperature *is rising* slightly each year because of increased amounts of carbon dioxide in the air.
Past progressive	The British *were preparing* for the attacks.
Future progressive	The doctor *will be seeing* more patients this afternoon than she expected.
Present perfect progressive	Professor Berz *has been finishing* her most recent novel for several months.
Past perfect progressive	I *had been composing* my letter of resignation for two hours when the telephone rang.
Future perfect progressive	By March 1, the state transportation department *will have been planning* the new highway to the airport for two years.

4. Sequence of Tenses

Almost any extended passage of English prose contains verbs in different tenses. You need to determine which tenses can logically follow one another, particularly in a sentence containing one or more dependent clauses. As the following sentences indicate, the relationships among tenses can sometimes be complicated.

Incorrect	When the mayor first died, her fellow citizens realized how much she contributed to the community, and since then, they collected money for a memorial.
Correct	When the mayor died, her fellow citizens realized how much she *had contributed* [before her death] to the community, and since then, they *have collected* [from that time to the present] money for a memorial.

a. Independent clauses

The sense of your sentence should be your guide as to the sequence of tenses in a sentence.

Main verb in present tense

Present + present

The motor *starts* when I *press* this button.

Main verb in past tense

Past + past

The motor *started* when I *pressed* this button.

Past + past perfect

The motor *started* when I *had pressed* this button.

Past + present

The motor *started* even though it *is* old.

Main verb in future tense

Future + present

The motor *will start* when I *press* this button.

Future + present perfect

The motor *will start* once I *have pressed* this button.

Main verb in present perfect tense

Present perfect + past

The motor *has started* because I *pressed* this button.

Main verb in past perfect tense

Past perfect + past

The motor *had started* because I *pressed* this button.

Main verb in future perfect tense

Future perfect + present

The motor *will have started* by the time I *press* this button.

Future perfect + present perfect

The motor *will have started* by the time I *have pressed* this button.

b. With infinitives

Use an infinitive in its present-tense form (*to* + base form of verb) unless it represents an action earlier than that of the main verb in the sentence. In that case, the correct form is the perfect infinitive (*to* + *have* + past participle of verb).

Incorrect   July 14, 1789, was a thrilling day *to have been* alive in Paris.

Correct   July 14, 1789, was a thrilling day *to be* alive in Paris.

[The sentence discusses the thrill of being alive *on* July 14, 1789, not before that date. The present infinitive is correct.]

c. With participles

When the action designated by a participle occurs at the same time as the action designated by the main verb in the sentence, use the present participle.

> *Believing* the defendant to have been a victim of circumstances, the jury found her not guilty.

> [The jury's belief and its decision occurred at the same time, so the present participle is correct. The perfect infinitive *to have been* appears in the sentence because the defendant's status as a victim preceded the jury's belief about her.]

When the action designated by a participle occurs before the action designated by the main verb, use the present perfect participle (*having* + past participle).

> *Having announced* their verdict, the jury members felt relieved.

> [First they announced their verdict, then they felt relieved. The present perfect participle is correct.]

5. Auxiliary Verbs

When forms of the verbs *have* and *be* are combined with principle parts of verbs to create the tenses of verbs, infinitives, and participles, they are called *auxiliary verbs*. The following are other auxiliary verbs.

a. Do

Like the verbs *have* and *be, do* may function both as a main verb (*I did the laundry this morning*) and as an auxiliary verb. In the latter role, it has three functions: to form negative constructions, to form interrogatives, and to add emphasis to a verb. The auxiliary *do* is always combined with the base form of a verb.

Negative construction	Kate's religion *does* not permit her to receive blood tranfusions.
Interrogative	*Did* she *share* her belief with the doctor?
Emphasis	I *do try* to see both sides of an issue like this, even when I find it perplexing.

b. Modal auxiliaries

Nine verbs in English are called *modal auxiliaries*. Each adds a specific shade of meaning to the main verb.

Can expresses ability:

Since my car is fixed, I *can* leave for California tomorrow.

Could expresses condition:

If my suitcase were packed, I *could* leave tomorrow.

May expresses possibility or permission:

I *may* leave tomorrow or I *may* not.

May I leave tomorrow, or would you prefer that I stay?

Might expresses weaker possibilities than *may:*

Depending on the weather, I *might* leave tomorrow.

Must expresses necessity:

I *must* leave tomorrow.

Ought to expresses obligation:

Jon called from Los Angeles to say that he needs my help. I *ought to* leave tomorrow.

Should expresses obligation:

> I *should* stop procrastinating and leave tomorrow.

Will expresses intention:

> I have put off this trip long enough. Tomorrow I *will* leave.

Would expresses condition:

> If I were to leave tomorrow, *would* you come with me?

Each modal auxiliary has only one form. It is therefore unaffected by the person or number of the subject.

> I *should* leave tomorrow.

> She *should* have left yesterday.

> They *should* be leaving soon.

6. Voice

Voice indicates whether the subject of the sentence is the actor in the sentence or is acted upon. In a sentence with a verb in the active voice, the subject performs the action that the verb describes:

> actor   action   recipient
> New Orleans *has inspired* writers for over two centuries.

In a sentence with a verb in the passive voice, on the other hand, the subject is acted upon by an actor that may or may not be identified in the sentence:

> recipient   action   actor
> Writers *have been inspired* by New Orleans for more than two centuries.

a. Forming passive verbs

The passive is created by combining the appropriate form of *be* and the past participle.

Present	I *am trusted* by you.
Past	I *was trusted* by you.
Future	I *will be trusted* by you.
Present perfect	I *have been trusted* by you.
Past perfect	I *had been trusted* by you.
Future perfect	I *will have been trusted* by you.

Passive verbs form the progressive by adding the appropriate progressive form of *be* to the past participle. Among the progressive forms in the passive voice, the present and past progressive are the most common.

Present progressive passive	I *am being trusted* by you.
Past progressive passive	I *was being trusted* by you.

b. Using active and passive verbs

We need passive verbs to express actions in which the actor is unimportant or cannot be identified. The passive verb effectively focuses attention on the action and the recipient of that action and de-emphasizes the unknown actors.

      recipient   action
Our apartment *was burglarized* yesterday.

When the actor in a sentence is known and may be significant, the active voice is usually preferable for two reasons. First, a passive verb always requires more words than an active verb to express the same idea. Second, a passive verb may de-emphasize or obscure an actor who should in fact be identified in a sentence, as in the following case:

Passive verb obscures actor	It *has* long *been asserted* that smoking is not necessarily harmful to one's health.
Active verb indicates actor	Tobacco companies *have* long *asserted* that cigarette smoking is not necessarily harmful to one's health.

7. Mood

Verbs express a speaker's or writer's attitude by what is called their *mood*.

a. Indicative mood

Use the indicative mood to state a fact or ask a question.

I *was sitting* next to Nancy.

Were you *sitting* nearby?

b. Imperative mood

Use the imperative mood in a command.

Sit next to Nancy, please.

c. Subjunctive

Use the subjunctive mood to express conditions contrary to fact and to state certain demands and requests. Subjunctive verb forms differ from indicative forms in only two ways. First, the present subjunctive uses the base form of the verb for all persons and numbers, *including the third-person singular,* whereas the indicative mood uses the *-s* form. Second, the past subjunctive form of the verb *be* is *were* for all persons and numbers.

Although used much less today than formerly, the subjunctive mood still surfaces in a number of idiomatic expressions (*Be that as it may, Far be it for me*) and in the following three specific situations.

Clauses beginning with if, as if, *or* as though, *and stating a condition contrary to fact*

If I *were* [not *was*] you, I would pay no attention to Steve's investment advice.
[In reality, I am not you.]

Steve confidently offers advice *as if* he *were* [not *was*] an experienced investor.
[In reality, he is not experienced.]

Clauses expressing a wish or desire

I wish your Hungarian cooking class *weren't* [not *wasn't*] already full.

Clauses beginning with that *and stating a demand, request, recommendation, or requirement*

I demand *that* I *be* [not *am*] allowed to address the council.

May I ask *that* my friends *be* [not *are*] recognized as well?

Chapter 18

Exercise 1 Verb Tenses

Underline the correct tenses of verbs, infinitives, and participles in the following sentences.

1. America's Progressive movement (spanned, had spanned) the years 1900 to 1917.

2. As a reaction to large-scale industrialism, during these years proposals (had emerged, were emerging) to correct the imbalance of power and make government more democratic.

3. (Fueling, having fueled) the Progressive momentum in his own term, President Theodore Roosevelt (endorsed, was endorsing) William Taft to succeed him and further his Progressive agenda.

4. However, Taft's conservatism (had proved, proved) (to divide, to have divided) more deeply the Republican party into supporters of big business, called Stalwarts, and supporters of progressivism, called Insurgents.

5. Taft's earlier consistent alignment with the Stalwarts (had prompted, prompted) Roosevelt to challenge his former endorsee's bid for the Republican party's 1912 presidential nomination.

6. (Failing, Having failed) to obtain his party's support, Roosevelt joined the Insurgents who (formed, had formed) the Progressive party, also termed the Bull Moose party.

7. Led mainly by midwestern Republicans, the Progressive party (became, was becoming) an influential force in national politics.

8. (Having run, Running) as the Progressive party's presidential candidate, Roosevelt successfully (turned, was turning) voters away from Republican Taft.

9. By (having split, splitting) the Republican vote, Roosevelt helped allow the election of Democrat Woodrow Wilson.

10. After Roosevelt (declined, had declined) the presidential nomination in 1916, the Progressives had no national candidate.

11. By 1917, the ranks of the Progressive party already (had dwindled, dwindled), so the party merged with the Prohibition party.

12. The goals that (had been proposed, were proposed) by the party—such as women's suffrage; medical and unemployment insurance; and public ownership of natural resources—did not come to be realized until later.

Chapter 18

Exercise 2 Modal Verbs

Insert a modal verb into each of the following sentences to create the meaning indicated.

1. Some people find that gardening _____ be an effective way to relieve stress. [ability]

2. If you _____ like to see whether tending plants _____ help you feel better after a busy day but you think your apartment doesn't have space for a garden, you _____ consider growing house-plants. [condition, condition, obligation]

3. Since different plants require different growing conditions, you _____ determine how bright, warm, and humid your home _____ be. [necessity, ability]

4. Some plants need frequent attention—trimming, watering, and fertilizing—so you _____ also decide how much work you want to invest in your plants. [obligation]

5. Although many people _____ be apprehensive about being first-time plant owners, certain plants _____ thrive in spite of neglect. [condition, ability]

6. You _____ be careful to choose plants suited to your surroundings; pathos and philodendrons _____ grow in fairly dark apartments, while cacti _____ have bright light but need very little attention or water. [obligation, intention, necessity]

7. You _____ place a schefflera or a diffenbachia in a room that gets indirect light; these plants _____ burn if they receive too much sun. [weak possibility, possibility]

8. If your apartment gets very little light, you _____ to think about installing plant lights. [obligation]

9. Special lamps are available, but you _____ buy ordinary fluorescent shop lights, which function as well as special plant lights and are much cheaper. [condition]

10. Once you have decided which plants _____ grow best in your home, you _____ figure out what sort of plant _____ look best in each spot. [ability, obligation, condition]

11. A spider plant _____ add interest to a window, since with little attention it _____ grow like a weed, sending off new plants in shoots. [condition, intention]

12. A cat _____ find a spider plant particularly tantalizing, so you _____ hang it out of reach. [intention, obligation]

13. If you _____ stand to watch its leaves drop off in the first weeks you own it, consider getting a ficus, or weeping fig. [ability]

14. The tree-like appearance of this plant _____ add depth to a room, and once it becomes acclimated to its new home, its leaves _____ grow back. [ability, obligation]

15. African violets are easier to grow than you _____ think, and with good artificial light, they _____ stay in bloom for months, brightening your room. [weak possibility, intention]

16. Whatever variety you choose, you _____ attend to the particular needs of your plants. [necessity]

17. A houseplant book _____ help until you learn how to care for your new plants. [ability]

Chapter 18

Exercise 3 Passive and Active Voice

Underline all passive verbs in the following sentences. If a sentence would be improved by using the active voice instead, revise it, making up likely actors if necessary.

1. William Blake was born in London in 1757, the same year that another mystical English poet, Christopher Smart, was arrested for praying in public in St. James Square.

2. By the time the age of twenty was reached by Blake, he had been apprenticed by his parents to James Basire, an engraver.

3. Blake was taught to copy monuments and buildings to be published as illustrations in books.

4. In this way, the skills of engraving and the knowledge of the publishing process in eighteenth-century London were acquired by Blake.

5. This knowledge was later used when his own books were created and were published by his own hand.

6. Like Smart, Blake was religious but unconventional.

7. Trouble with the authorities was run into because of the unorthodox attitudes that were held.

8. In Blake's most famous engraved book, *The Marriage of Heaven and Hell,* the philosophy against organized religion and arbitrary authority that was expressed by Blake throughout his life is presented eloquently.

Chapter *18*

Exercise 4 Verb Mood

Correct the following sentences by changing verbs in the indicative mood to the subjunctive mood where necessary.

1. At breakfast, Jane announced, "I wish I could say this wasn't true, but last night I got a speeding ticket."

2. Mary, her roommate, commented, "You don't sound as though it was your fault."

3. "It wasn't as if I was doing anything really bad," Jane said defensively.

4. "I was only going 45 in a 25 mph zone because I had to hurry if I was going to get to my aerobics class on time."

5. "The officer seemed as though he was waiting just for me," Jane complained.

6. "I demanded that I was allowed to keep my license, but the officer looked at me as if I was asking for something unreasonable." She concluded, "If you were I, would you fight it in court?"

7. "If I was you," replied Mary, "I'd buy a bicycle."

19

Sentence Fragments, Comma Splices, Fused Sentences

Avoid breaking sentences into fragments or incorrectly joining them. Such errors not only violate rules of grammatical usage but also distract and confuse your reader.

1. Types of Sentence Fragments

When part of a sentence is punctuated as if it were a complete sentence, it is a *sentence fragment*.

a. Dependent clause as fragment

Either join a dependent clause to the sentence of which it is logically a part or rewrite it as an independent clause.

Fragment
Often I stay up late in my room, studying, writing, or thinking about the future. While all the other students in the dorm are asleep.

Correct
Often I stay up late in my room, studying, writing, or thinking about the future while all the other students in the dorm are asleep.

Notice that the correction retains the precise connection between the two clauses. This revision does not:

Correct but weak
Often I stay up late in my room, studying, writing, or thinking about the future. All the other students in the dorm are asleep.

b. Participial phrase as fragment

A participial phrase functions as an adjective and must be joined to the sentence containing the noun or pronoun that it modifies.

Fragment	Reporters and secretaries were rushing all around the office. Running up and down the aisles, conferring with the editors, and talking in small groups.
Correct	Reporters and secretaries were rushing all around the office, running up and down the aisles, conferring with the editors, and talking in small groups.
Fragment	I stepped into the chaotic room in search of a desk with my name on it. Having already decided that working here would be an adventure.
Correct	I stepped into the chaotic room in search of a desk with my name on it, having already decided that working here would be an adventure.

c. Infinitive phrase as fragment

An infinitive phrase, *to* plus a verb form, cannot stand alone.

Fragment	After a long discussion, I finally received permission from my parents. To spend the summer with El Centro de Paz, a work project in Mexico.
Correct	After a long discussion, I finally received permission from my parents to spend the summer with El Centro de Paz, a work project in Mexico.

d. Prepositional phrase as fragment

A preposition (such as *at, for, in, over, through,* or *with*), its object, and any modifiers constitute a prepositional phrase. A prepositional phrase modifies another word in a sentence and must be joined to the sentence containing that word.

Fragment	Many people pour chemicals on their lawns each summer. Without a thought about the possible hazards of these concoctions.
Correct	Many people pour chemicals on their lawns each summer without a thought about the possible hazards of these concoctions.

In some cases, you may be able to expand a prepositional phrase into a full sentence.

Correct	Many people pour chemicals on their lawns each summer. They don't think about the possible hazards of these concoctions.

e. Appositive phrase as fragment

An appositive phrase is typically a noun phrase that describes or explains another noun or pronoun. Such a phrase must be linked to the word it describes, usually with a comma or a dash.

Fragment	The physician recognized the signs of shock in the patient. Elevated pulse rate, low blood pressure, and clammy skin.
Correct	The physician recognized the signs of shock in the patient— elevated pulse rate, low blood pressure, and clammy skin.

An appositive may contain within it a dependent clause.

Fragment	No one could identify the victim. A woman in her late twenties who had staggered into the hospital before collapsing.

| Correct | No one could identify the victim, a woman in her late twenties who had staggered into the hospital before collapsing. |

Sometimes you can rewrite an appositive as an independent clause or full sentence.

| Correct | No one could identify the victim. A woman in her late twenties, she had staggered into the hospital before collapsing. |

2. Comma Splices

A comma splice, sometimes called a comma fault, occurs when two independent clauses are joined only with a comma. Comma splices can distract and confuse the reader.

> In the doorway stood my nephew, soaked from the rain, the dog lay at his feet.

a. Use a period to divide the clauses into separate sentences

This strategy works well when a transitional word, phrase, or clause is present to express the relationship between the two sentences that you create.

| Comma splice | There was an extremely heavy rain on Monday night, after the storm had passed, the streams were overflowing. |

| Correct | There was an extremely heavy rain on Monday night. After the storm had passed, the streams were overflowing. |

b. Use a semicolon

Use a semicolon by itself when the two independent clauses are so closely related that you do not need to state their relationship explicitly.

Comma splice	Gambling is like a drug, after a while the gambler finds it impossible to stop.
Correct	Gambling is like a drug; after a while the gambler finds it impossible to stop.

The semicolon must be preceded and followed by an independent clause.

When two independent clauses are linked by a conjunctive adverb such as *consequently, however, moreover, nonetheless, then,* or *therefore,* or by a transitional phrase like *as a result, for example,* or *on the other hand,* a semicolon is required.

Comma splice	To most of the economists at the conference, a rise in interest rates seemed inevitable, however, three of the experts predicted the opposite.
Correct	To most of the economists at the conference, a rise in interest rates seemed inevitable; however, three of the experts predicted the opposite.

As an alternative, two independent clauses linked by a conjunctive adverb or a transitional phrase may be divided into separate sentences.

Note that a conjunctive adverb need not come first in a clause. You may insert it in a number of places. It is preceded or followed by a semicolon only when it serves as the connection between two independent clauses.

Incorrect	It seems to me; however, that I might be wrong.
Correct	It seems to me, however, that I might be wrong.

c. Use a coordinating conjunction

Use a coordinating conjunction (*and, but, nor, or, so, yet*) to connect two independent clauses when you wish to give them equal emphasis.

| Comma splice | The parks in this city are very poorly maintained, the two public swimming pools are in bad condition as well. |
| Correct | The parks in this city are very poorly maintained, and the two public swimming pools are in bad condition as well. |

d. Use a subordinating conjunction or a relative pronoun

If the two independent clauses are unequal in importance, you may be able to correct the comma splice by subordinating one clause with a subordinating conjunction (such as *after, although, because, since, while, whereas,* or *when*) or with a relative pronoun (such as *that, which,* and *who*).

| Comma splice | Marjorie has stopped lending her friend money, she doesn't trust him any longer. |
| Correct | Marjorie has stopped lending her friend money, because she doesn't trust him any longer. |

e. Acceptable comma splices

Short, parallel independent clauses can sometimes be joined only with commas, particularly in narratives.

The sky darkened, the wind blew, the cold rain began to fall.

3. Fused Sentences

A fused sentence is one in which two independent clauses are joined with no punctuation between them. This error makes your reader's task of deciphering your sentence extremely difficult.

| Fused | The senate passed the bill only after long hours of debate both sides had strong feelings about the measure. |

To correct a fused sentence, use any of the strategies offered for correcting comma splices.

Chapter *19*

Exercise 1 Sentence Fragments

Underline the sentence fragments in the following passage. Then revise the passage to eliminate those errors. Be prepared to discuss the cause of each fragment.

What people eat depends a great deal on where and when they live. In part because of the availability of certain foods. And because food is connected with conventions and norms. Religious beliefs also affect diet. For example, the restriction for Orthodox Jews against eating meat and dairy products at the same meal. While for many years Catholics were not allowed to eat meat on Friday. What is really interesting is what people *will* eat. Without thinking it strange at all. Some foods that people ate in the past seeming particularly strange. A good example is cockentrice, a medieval delicacy made up of half a suckling pig and half a chicken, sewn together, baked, and decorated. Obviously, tastes change over time. Anyone who protests that tastes are more discriminating in this century needs to reconsider that claim. To take a closer look at other cultures. Eating habits vary greatly in different parts of the world. In some places, monkey brains being a delicacy. As are insects. "There's more than one way to skin a cat" is just a figure of speech, unless you live in Asia. Visitors to America, too, are surprised by variations in diet. Rattlesnake, pig lips, and raw shrimp. However, even entire groups of people may learn to appreciate foods that once seemed strange to them. Accepting that other cultures may have something worthwhile to offer to their dinner tables. Just as children learn to develop a taste for "adult" foods. There may be limits, though. Whether soy ice cream or sesame burgers become popular enough to be served at fast-food chains. Another old expression, "You are what you eat," a little more interesting and a little more ominous all the time.

231

Chapter 19
Exercise 2 Comma Splices and Fused Sentences

Label comma splices (CS) and fused sentences (FS) wherever they appear in the following passage. Use a variety of techniques to correct them.

How many different kinds of computers are there? The answer to this question may come as a surprise to the average person, there is really only one: the Von Neuman machine. In the 1940s, John Von Neuman defined the "stored program computer" it must have some means of reading and writing an unlimited amount of data and some kind of memory, in addition it must have what is now called a central processing unit, or CPU, this has two functions. First, the CPU performs arithmetic and logical calculations, second, it chooses between possible actions on the basis of those calculations. Every modern computer is based on this definition, the differences among computers arising from how these functions are implemented. In the early days, for instance, input and output were done on punched cards. Each card was called a record, it contained either one piece of data or one instruction (such as "add the last two numbers") for the CPU. A modern computer reads and writes directly to memory, to some sort of storage like a floppy disk, possibly it uses a keyboard and printer. Another difference is that the CPU of an older computer was all "hardware," however, most modern computers implement the calculating section in hardware but the control section in "firmware." A firmware control section is like a little computer in itself. It has a memory, one program is permanently stored in it. This program tells the computer to get the next instruction or piece of data from the input medium and perform the appropriate calculations then it tests the results to determine what comes next. Different computer designs arise from the same motives that govern most marketing principles, such as a desire to appeal to different consumers. A firmware control section, for instance, may not run as quickly as a hardware one but contains fewer parts this makes it cheaper to produce. Aside from such distinctions, however, no one has yet been able to improve on the basic Von Neuman definition of a computer probably no one ever will.

Chapter *19*

Exercise 3 Fragments, Comma Splices, and Fused Sentences

Label the fragments (FR), comma splices (CS), and fused sentences (FS) in the following passage. Rewrite the passage to correct the errors, using a variety of methods.

The peach is believed to be native to China however it has the species name *persica*. Because it was introduced to Europe from Persia, now called Iran. The Spaniards brought the peach to Florida in the sixteenth century, it adapts well and grows easily from its seeds, the English even found wild peaches growing in Virginia. Worldwide, only the apple and the pear are more important than the peach. It grows in temperate climates. The United States, the leading grower, producing about one-fifth of the world's total output. California accounts for more than half of the production in the United States. Peaches are divided into two basic types, freestone or clingstone, the categories are based on the difficulty of removing the stone or pit from the flesh. The trees may live only twenty to thirty years, they are often planted as fillers in apple orchards. Because apple trees survive much longer. After ten years some growers destroy the peach trees around the eighth or ninth year the peak period of fruit production occurs. Most varieties produce more fruit than the trees can support. Some natural pruning occurs about a month to six weeks after the trees have bloomed fully, however, hand pruning must supplement this natural thinning. If, as the growers desire, the fruit is to reach a large size. The nectarine with its smooth skin may seem to be a very different fruit. It is a divergent form, however, related to the peach.

20 *Punctuation*

If you are unsure whether or not to punctuate and cannot identify a rule that applies, use your best judgment. Modern usage tends toward less punctuation rather than more.

1. The Period

a. After a declarative or mildly imperative sentence

A declarative sentence, like this one, ends with a period.

Don't forget to end a mild command with a period, too.

Never combine a period at the end of a sentence with another punctuation mark.

Incorrect	The train leaves every day at 7:25 A.M..
Correct	The train leaves every day at 7:25 A.M.

Similarly, if a declarative sentence ends with a quotation, the final punctuation within the quotation marks suffices for the entire sentence.

Incorrect	Michael looked at me and said, "I never received your letter.".
Correct	Michael looked at me and said, "I never received your letter."

b. After an indirect question or a polite request

I wonder how many people would know that this is an indirect question and must end with a period, not a question mark.

Will you please remember to use a question mark only after a direct question.

c. With abbreviations

Many abbreviations include or are followed by periods.

Mr.   Ms.   Rev.   Ph.D.   etc.   Inc.

Some abbreviations, like the U.S. Postal Service abbreviations for states, are not followed by periods: *IL, LA, NY, WA*. Many organizations and agencies are represented by their initials without periods: *CBS, FAA, NAACP*. Periods are also not used with acronyms (abbreviations spoken as words): *MADD* (Mothers against Drunk Driving), *DOS* (disk operating system).

d. With ellipses

Three periods—with spaces before, between, and after them—are ellipsis marks; use them to indicate the omission of a word or words from a quoted passage. If the omitted words come at the end of a sentence, do not leave a space before the first period, but do add a fourth period to end the sentence.

> "I pledge allegiance to the flag . . . and to the Republic for which it stands. . . ."

e. In dialogue

Occasionally you may use three (or, at the end of a sentence, four) periods in writing dialogue to indicate hesitation and pauses.

> "I just can't remember the details. . . ." Judy drifted off in midsentence, trying to concentrate.

2. The Question Mark

a. After direct questions or questions in a series

> Isn't this the kind of question that must end with a question mark?

> Shouldn't you use a question mark at the end of this question? And this one? And what about this one?

If a question ends with an abbreviation that includes a period, the question mark follows the period.

> Did the invitation say R.S.V.P.?

In other situations, however, do not combine a question mark with other punctuation marks.

> Did you say, "I'm not going to the party"?

b. To indicate doubtful information

You may use a question mark in parentheses to indicate that the information in a sentence is of doubtful accuracy.

Hippocrates was born on the island of Cos in 460 (?) B.C.

Do not use a question mark in parentheses to be sarcastic; find words to convey your feelings instead.

3. The Exclamation Point

Use exclamation points sparingly. An exclamation point is appropriate only after those statements, commands, or interjections that would be given unusual emphasis if spoken.

I will *not* go to the party with your cousin!

If an emphatic statement ends with an abbreviation that contains a period, the exclamation point follows the period.

I refuse to leave for the party before 1:00 P.M.!

4. The Comma

A primary function of the comma is to make a sentence clear. Use commas to prevent misreading—to separate words that your reader might erroneously group together.

a. With a coordinating conjunction to separate independent clauses

I failed German in my senior year of high school, *and* I did not want to study any other language for a long time.

Very short independent clauses need not be separated by a comma.

The bell rang and everyone left.

b. To set off an introductory element

An introductory dependent clause is always set off with a comma.

Whenever I read about the nineteenth century, I am struck by the sufferings of the poor.

Use a comma after most introductory phrases, particularly if they are longer than a few words.

> After seeing the poverty of the working-class people, Elizabeth Gaskell wrote several protest novels.

c. To separate elements in a series

Words, phrases, or clauses in a series should be separated by commas.

> Books, papers, and photographs were strewn about the room.

> If you feel faint, if your vision becomes blurred, or if you have difficulty breathing, discontinue this medication.

> Water flooded over the riverbanks, across the road, and into the basements of nearby homes.

Some writers omit the comma before the last time in a series, but its use is preferred. Omitting it can cause misreading.

> The three congressional priorities are nuclear disarmament, the curtailment of agricultural trade and aid to underdeveloped countries. [Without a comma before *and*, *aid* can be read as an object of *curtailment*.]

d. With coordinate modifiers

Adjectives modifying the same noun should be separated by commas if they are coordinate, that is, if they could be joined by *and* without distorting the meaning of the sentence.

> Bus lines provide *inexpensive, efficient* transportation.

Sometimes an adjective is so closely linked with the noun that it is considered part of the noun. Such an adjective is not coordinate and should not be set off by a comma.

> The Paynes bought a *spacious summer home.*

e. To set off a nonrestrictive modifier

A dependent clause, participial phrase, or appositive is *nonrestrictive* when it can be omitted without changing the main idea of the sentence. A nonrestrictive modifier gives additional information about the noun to which it refers. A restrictive modifier, on the other hand, restricts the meaning of the word it modifies to one particular group or thing. It if is omitted, the main idea of the sentence changes.

Nonrestrictive	My faculty adviser, *who had to sign the program card,* was hard to find. [Without the clause, the meaning of the sentence would still be clear.]
Restrictive	Faculty advisers *who are never in their offices* make registration difficult. [The statement refers only to a certain kind of faculty adviser.]

Use two commas to set off a nonrestrictive modifier in the middle of a sentence; use one comma if the modifier is at the beginning or end of the sentence.

The meaning of a sentence may be altered by the addition or omission of commas.

The board sent questionnaires to all members, who are on Social Security. [Nonrestrictive clause. The sentence implies that all members are on Social Security.]

The board sent questionnaires to all members who are on Social Security. [Restrictive clause. The sentence implies that the questionnaire was sent to only some members, those on Social Security.]

In relative clauses beginning with *that* or *which,* use *that* in restrictive clauses, *which* in nonrestrictive.

f. To set off parenthetic elements

Parenthetic is a general term describing explanatory words and phrases that interrupt the normal sentence pattern to supply additional, but not essential, information. Set off parenthetic elements by commas (or in some cases by parentheses or dashes).

Adjectives in normal position	Two *tired* and *hungry* boys wandered into camp.
Adjectives as parenthetic element	Two boys, *tired* and *hungry,* wandered into camp.
Clause as parenthetic element	Two boys, *who were tired and hungry,* wandered into camp.

Conjunctive adverbs (such as *consequently, furthermore, however, moreover, nonetheless,* and *therefore*) and transitional phrases (such as *for example, as a result,* and *on the other hand*) frequently function as parenthetic elements. Set them off with commas when they are in the middle of a sentence and with a single comma when they are at the end.

g. To set off absolute phrases

An absolute phrase typically consists of a noun and a participle or complement. Set it off with commas.

> *The hurricane having passed,* workers began to clear debris from the roads.

h. In comparative and contrastive constructions

Use commas to separate some idiomatic coordinate constructions involving a comparison: *the more . . . , the more . . .* and *the more . . . , the less. . . .*

> *The older* the tree, *the weaker* its resistance to disease.

Coordinate words or phrases that are contrasted are often also separated by a comma.

> We are *a contentious group,* but not *a belligerent one.*

i. With interjections, direct address, and tag questions

Set off with commas interjections and nouns used as terms of direct address.

> Ms. Kuhn, may I speak frankly?

Set off with a comma an elliptical question, or tag question, attached to the end of a related statement.

> You can't defend this proposal, *can you?*

j. With dates, addresses, place names, and numbers

If only one element in a date (month and day, or month and year), place name, or address (number and street) appears in a sentence, do not use a comma.

> April 4 is Sandy's birthday.

Set off multiple elements by commas.

Sandy was born on Monday, April 4, 1960, in Scranton, Pennsylvania.

Do not use a comma when you invert a date: *7 December 1941*. Do not use commas in numbers referring to pages, years, or addresses.

On page 2522 of my almanac is a calendar for all the years from 1801 to the present.

k. With direct quotations

The words used to identify the speaker of a quotation are set off by commas in a direct quotation.

"When I was in Africa," Brad said, "I learned a great deal about the plight of elephants."

When the quotation contains two independent clauses, use a semicolon or period after the words identifying the speaker to prevent a comma splice.

"When I was in Africa, I learned a great deal about the plight of elephants," Brad said; "their future depends on other nations."

Do not use a comma in an indirect quotation.

Brad said that most countries have now banned the importation of ivory.

l. Misuse of the comma

Be especially careful to avoid the following incorrect uses of commas.

Comma erroneously separates subject and verb

Ted's ability to solve the most complicated of problems, never failed to impress his co-workers.

Comma erroneously precedes first element of a series

For lunch I usually have, a sandwich, some fruit, and milk.

Comma erroneously follows last element in a series

New Jersey, Rhode Island, and Massachusetts, were the most densely populated states as of the last census.

Comma erroneously divides indirect quotation

During chapel the minister announced, that the choir would sing Handel's *Messiah* for Easter.

Comma erroneously splits idiomatic construction

Joy is so tall, that she may well break the school's record for rebounds.

5. The Semicolon

a. To connect independent clauses not linked by a coordinating conjunction

Use a semicolon in place of a comma and coordinating conjunction when two independent clauses are closely related.

I'm not saying that these stories are untrue; I'm just a bit doubtful about your source.

Use a semicolon when two independent clauses are linked by a conjunctive adverb such as *consequently* or *however*.

Our plan was to sail from Naples to New York; *however,* an emergency at home forced us to fly back.

If you use a comma rather than a semicolon in the two preceding examples, a comma splice will result.

b. To separate elements in a series

When elements in a series contain internal commas, use semicolons to separate them clearly.

Confusing	The Parents' Day discussion was led by Mr. Joseph, the chaplain, Ms. Smith, a French instructor, the dean, and his assistant.
Clear	The Parents' Day discussion was led by Mr. Joseph, the chaplain; Ms. Smith, a French instructor; the dean; and his assistant.

6. Quotation Marks

a. To enclose direct quotation

Use quotation marks to enclose direct quotation but not indirect quotation.

Indirect	He said that he would call.
Direct	He said, "I will call."

If a quotation consists of several uninterrupted sentences, use one set of quotation marks to enclose the entire quotation. If a quotation consists of several paragraphs, put quotation marks at the beginning of each paragraph and at the end of the last paragraph.

At the end of a quotation, place a period or comma inside the quotation marks; place a semicolon or colon outside.

"Quick," said my cousin, "hand me the flashlight."

The bride and groom in the film said, "I do"; the audience cheered.

I have only one comment when you say, "All people are equal": I wish it were true.

Place a question mark or exclamation point inside the quotation mark if it applies to the quotation only, and outside if it applies to the whole sentence.

Did the invitation say "R.S.V.P."?

He called irritably, "Move over!"

Use single quotation marks to enclose a quotation within a quotation.

The lecture began, "As Proust said, 'Any mental activity is easy if it need not take reality into account.' "

b. To indicate titles of works

Use quotation marks for titles of articles, short stories, short poems, songs, chapters, lectures, speeches, and individual episodes of radio and television shows.

The titles of books, plays, long poems, pamphlets, periodicals, films, radio and television programs, and major works of opera, dance, and music are represented by italics or, on a typewriter, by underlining.

c. To enclose words defined in the text

The first time you define an unfamiliar word or phrase in your writing, use quotation marks to enclose it. To refer to a word as such, use italics (or underlining) rather than quotation marks: the word *word*.

d. Misuse of quotation marks

Whenever you enclose a text in quotation marks, be careful that you not make any changes in it. And never use quotation marks to enclose material that you have paraphrased.

Avoid using quotation marks as an implicit apology for slang or other questionable usages: *That comedian's monologue really "slayed" me.* If you have to apologize for a word, don't use it.

7. The Apostrophe
a. To indicate the possessive case

All singular nouns and indefinite pronouns, including those that already end in -*s,* form the possessive by adding -*'s:* a *child's* toy, *Agnes's* clarinet.

An exception to the rule exists only when an awkward-sounding proper noun would result. In those instances, form the possessive by adding just an apostrophe: *Moses'* life, *Euripides'* plays.

All plural nouns that do not end in -*s* also form the possessive by adding -*'s: children's* games, two *moose's* antlers.

All plural nouns that end in -*s* form the possessive by adding the apostrophe alone: in two *hours'* time, the *Kennedys'* estate.

Compound nouns and pronouns form the possessive by adding -*'s* to the final word: someone *else's* book, my *sister-in-law's* visit.

In a phrase indicating joint possession, the last noun takes the possessive form; in one indicating individual possession, each noun takes the possessive form: *Marshall and Ward's* Minneapolis branch; *John's, Pamela's,* and *Harold's* separate claims.

The personal pronouns never take an apostrophe, even though their possessive forms end in -*s: his, hers, its, ours, yours, theirs.*

b. To form contractions

Use an apostrophe to indicate omissions in contracted words and dates: *it's* (it is), *class of '94* (class of 1994).

c. To form the plurals of letters and numbers

Form the plurals of letters and numerals by adding -'s: Her *w's* were like my *m's,* and her *6's* resembled *G's.*

Form the plural of a word considered as a word in the same way: His conversation is too full of *you know's.*

8. Other Punctuation Marks

a. The colon

Use the colon primarily to introduce a formal enumeration or list, a quotation, or an explanatory statement.

Consider these three viewpoints: political, economic, and social.

The sentence preceding the colon should be grammatically complete.

Incorrect	We provide: fishing permit, rod, hooks, bait, and boat.
Correct	We provide fishing permit, rod, hooks, bait, and boat.

You may also use the colon between two independent clauses when the second clause explains or develops the first.

b. The dash

On a typewriter, a dash consists of two hyphens with no spaces before, between, or after them.

When an appositive or parenthetic element contains commas, set it off with dashes.

Three works of art—a watercolor, an oil, and a silk-screen print—hung on the wall.

When a parenthetic element consists of an independent clause, set it off with dashes (or parentheses) rather than commas.

By the time the speech was over—it lasted two hours—most of the audience was asleep.

When a sentence begins with a series or list, you may use a dash to link it with the statement that follows.

Birth, life, death—this is the cycle from which no one escapes.

You may occasionally use a dash to indicate a sharp and perhaps unexpected turn of thought in a sentence. Parenthetic elements set off with dashes receive special emphasis. Be careful to use the dash sparingly, since its overuse weakens its effectiveness.

c. Parentheses

Use parentheses to enclose or set off explanatory or supplementary material. Unlike commas, parentheses usually enclose material that is less closely related in meaning or structure to the rest of the sentence. They provide you with an opportunity to express your comments or asides. Unlike dashes, parentheses reduce rather than increase dramatic effect.

d. Brackets

Use brackets to enclose a word or words inserted into a quotation by the person quoting it in order to comment on the quotation or provide an explanation of a word or phrase in it that would otherwise be unclear.

The program director said, "Everyone in the metropolitan area [of Chicago] will welcome the opening of the newest facility."

Chapter *20*

Exercise 1 End Punctuation

Supply the appropriate punctuation at the end of each sentence in the following passage.

Many people ask themselves what will happen in the future Psychics try to answer the question not only of "what" but of "when" Their predictions are not always accurate, but they are often interesting, aren't they In response to some predictions, we can only exclaim, "Where do they get such ideas" For example, one psychic regularly focuses on the future of a whole state This person actually predicted that Florida would become one huge nudist colony Psychics have different ways of asking what the future will bring What the crystal ball says and what is revealed in coffee grounds are two methods Most psychics are not able to make a living from their predictions, so the question is how they support themselves Is it surprising that one psychic is a mortician, another is a hairdresser, and a third is a psychiatrist The last of these prefers to remain anonymous and is known only as Dr. N

Chapter 20

Exercise 2   Commas: Restrictive and Nonrestrictive Modifiers

Insert commas where they are needed in the following sentences to set off nonrestrictive modifiers. In doubtful cases, explain the two possible meanings of the sentences.

1. Victoria who was born in 1819 was destined to become one of the longest-ruling monarchs in modern history.
2. Victoria's father Edward also known as the Duke of Kent was the third son of the mad English king George III.
3. Her mother who was also named Victoria was the Princess of Saxe-Coburg, Dowager Princess of Leiningen.
4. Because the Duke of Kent was out of favor with the rest of the royal family, Parliament would not grant him an increase in his royal stipend sufficient to cover his expenses which were extravagant.
5. Therefore, the couple trying to save money lived abroad.
6. However, they returned to England in time for Victoria's birth because she was near in line to the throne, and her parents wanted to appease people who claimed she was not sufficiently English to rule.
7. The new princess was named at her christening ceremony which was held on June 24, 1819.
8. Because she was a royal princess and in line for the throne, her name had to be approved by the Prince of Wales who was the Prince Regent during his father's confinement for madness.
9. The princess was raised by her mother; her mother's confidant, John Conroy; and her nurse-governess under a mode of education that was called the Kensington system.
10. Under the Kensington system, the little princess who was never left alone was not allowed to see any person except in the presence of her mother, Conroy, or Lehzen.
11. The princess had no playmates except for Conroy's children whom she did not like.
12. It was not until William IV died, on June 19, 1837, that Victoria stepped into the role that was her birthright and took over the duties of state which she fulfilled admirably during her life.

Chapter 20
Exercise 3 Commas

Add commas where needed in the following sentences. Be prepared to explain your punctuation according to the rules.

That society influences literature is certainly obvious. Equally true however is that literature at times has had far-reaching profound social effects. For example Dickens who wrote in nineteenth-century England helped to rouse public outcry against prison conditions and treatment of the poor. In America one novel that worked as a catalyst for social change was Upton Sinclair's *The Jungle*. The book which was published in 1906 traces the experiences of a worker living in Packingtown a reference to the Chicago Illinois stockyards. Jurvis the main character lives in squalor works under dangerous conditions and encounters tragedy upon tragedy. Although Sinclair intended readers to respond humanely to the plight of such workers the main result of his book was the passage that year of the Meat Inspection Act. With its gruesome descriptions of the quality of the meat itself (diseased animals, filthy working areas and food contaminated with many disgusting things) the book upset people so much that it led to further investigations. The meat-packing industry protested but many journalists took up the cause. The tone of the journalists' allegations is exemplified in a 1906 issue of the *New York Evening Post* which quipped "Mary had a little lamb, and when she saw it sicken, she shipped it off to Packingtown, and now it's labeled 'chicken.' " That year also saw the passage of the Food and Drug Act. *The Jungle* is the most famous literary example of a tradition begun around the turn of the century of American muckrakers a term applied in 1906 by Theodore Roosevelt to social reformers who exposed social and political problems.

Chapter 20

Exercise 4 Semicolons

Some of the following sentences are correct as they stand. In the others, insert semicolons where they should appear.

1. There is a lot to do when you are planning to move, whether you plan to travel to a new city or just across town, moving takes time, care, and organization.

2. The first step is finding a new place to live, and it can be frustrating, because you have to reach a compromise between what you can live with and what you can't live without.

3. After you have arranged for a new home, the work really begins, you will have to start planning for the move itself.

4. Packing will almost always take longer than you expect it to, therefore, allow yourself extra time.

5. You can buy boxes from moving companies, you can also get them free at most grocery and liquor stores.

6. Inspect carefully any secondhand box, however, since it may carry insects as well as your possessions to your new home.

7. Packing glassware in newspaper is an inexpensive way to protect it from breaking, so is wrapping pictures in sheets and blankets.

8. If you pack books in brown paper sacks, the resulting packages will be compact and easy to stack, they will also be light enough to handle easily.

9. It is always better to have a number of light cartons than just a few heavy ones, boxes, as you probably know, get heavy quickly when you have to carry a lot of them.

10. If you are moving on the first or the fifteenth of the month, when everyone else wants to move, rental trucks may be hard to come by, therefore, it's a good idea to arrange well in advance for whatever transportation you need for your move.

11. Before you move, change your address with the post office, notify your credit-card companies, utilities, and bank, and, whether you have car insurance, renter's insurance, or both, let the company know you are relocating.

12. If you rent a truck, you may also want to rent furniture pads, they can be wrapped around large pieces of furniture to help prevent chips and scratches.

13. In order to get your security deposit back, clean the insides of cupboards, the refrigerator, and the oven, mop the floors, dust the floorboards, if you have them, and, in general, make sure that the place looks at least as good as when you first moved in.

14. Moving, even to the place of your dreams, is never easy, nonetheless, with some planning and care, at least it doesn't have to be a nightmare.

Chapter 20
Exercise 5   Punctuation

Insert quotation marks, apostrophes, and other appropriate punctuation where necessary in the following sentences.

1. As the first hitter stepped into the batters box, he asked the catcher Whos the new pitcher youve got today

2. His name is Marquardt the catcher replied and youd better watch out. Hes throwing a little wild today.

3. What do you mean by 'a little wild' the now-disconcerted batter asked, as the pitchers first offering sped directly over the plate into the waiting catchers glove.

4. The catcher smiled at the fans roar from the bleachers, saying Oh, nothing really. Were working on his control problems. His change-ups are as hard as most pitchers fastballs, but he cant seem to keep them over the plate.

5. The catcher continued, not entirely oblivious to the opposing hitters concern, You mightve read about him. When he was in the Minors, he was featured in an article called Demon Pitchers in *Baseball Monthly*. But dont worry. We havent ever proved that he hit a batter on purpose.

6. The batter, now staring openly at the catcher, didnt notice the next ball sail over the plate.

7. Strike two the umpire shouted Id watch the ball if I were you. If you paid as much attention to the game as you do to your conversation, you wouldnt have let that one slide by.

8. Wait a minute. You didnt call that a strike, did you the batter protested. That was so far inside, I had to jump out of the way.

9. What in the world is going on out there wondered the manager as the next throw, a fastball down the center of the strike zone, sent the batter leaping out of the way.

10. Strike three! yelled the umpire, but he was hardly audible over the crowds shouts.

11. Youre out screamed the umpire. The batter walked back slowly to the dugout, accompanied by the audiences hoots and jeers.

12. The catcher smiled as the next hitter stepped into the batter box. Could anyone hear him say, Youd better watch this new guy. Hes throwing a little wild today

Chapter 20

Exercise 6 Punctuation

Insert appropriate punctuation where it is needed in the following sentences. The punctuation that has already been supplied to guide you is correct.

Children all over the world have been raised on tales of mythical beasts creatures that seem to capture adults imaginations as well. The beasts are often mixtures of two or more animals either real or fantastic. In particular varieties of serpents seem to have a powerful hold over the human imagination. The chimera a term originally used to refer to a composite of a lion, a goat, and a serpent has come to stand for, as *The American Heritage Dictionary* says "a creation of the imagination" Other serpent monsters include Naga a many-headed snake; Hydra, a serpent or dragon with seven heads and the Basilisk, which has the body of a serpent and the head and claws of a bird. Dragons are closely related to serpents they are interchangeable at times—and have appealed to science fiction writers and other producers of popular culture. Most monsters combine a formidable strength and ferocity. A number of creatures are mixtures of humans and animals the familiar Mermaid, the seductive Siren mixture of bird and woman, the horse-man Centaur and the Minotaur a man with a bulls head. Most of these beings have specific qualities in the myths in which they originally appeared and they assume the same roles in more recent stories. Occasionally, a person might come across (in literature, of course a creature that seems particularly farfetched. Can you picture an Amemait, a combination of lion, crocodile, and hippopotamus Usually these monsters symbolize something that must be defeated by human will, creativity and strength the evil in the world or perhaps more importantly, qualities of human nature itself that align people with animals and must be conquered and civilized.

Chapter 20

Exercise 7 Punctuation

Insert appropriate punctuation where it is needed in the following sentences. The punctuation that has already been supplied to guide you is correct.

Most people use euphemisms for one thing or another often as a way of protecting, or as an attempt to protect the feelings of others. *Crippled* for example, has been replaced by the less pejorative *handicapped* or *disabled* Euphemisms used in this way differ from those intended to deceive people or avoid responsibility. The euphemisms—or "doublespeak," as such language is sometimes called that present the most danger to the public are the ones associated with politics and the military dangerous because they mask the magnitude and consequences of actions and they allow the people who make decisions to avoid taking responsibility for them. Some of these terms are chilling such as *friendly fire, incontinent ordnance* and *misadventure* all actual terms used to refer to the accidental bombing of our side by our side. The term *exchange* for "war" obviously neutralizes an action that is not neutral as does *incursion* for "invasion." Edwin Newman writes in *Strictly Speaking* "There were official objections to our calling [the 1971 invasion of Laos] an invasion, evidently in the belief that incursion implied something softer than invasion. . ." Metaphors can also act as euphemisms when politicians speak of *war games* and *playing hardball* they effectively mask the implications of the terms, with the result that military aggression—whether justified or not sounds like healthy competition or a childs game. An extreme example the horrifying removal of negative connotations is epitomized in the Nazi term for the execution of millions of people the Final Solution.

21　　*Spelling*

Most readers expect accurate spelling and, fairly or not, they will regard your spelling mistakes as indications of sloppiness or indifference. Like so many other aspects of writing, then, good spelling has a rhetorical function: it helps you to establish a persona characterized by precision and carefulness. Learn to look for trouble spots in words and concentrate on them—and keep a dictionary nearby.

1. Similar Words Frequently Confused

Many spelling errors involve words that look or sound similar or, even more problematic, have similar meanings. Here is a partial list, to give you an idea of what to look for:

accept	receive
except	aside from
berth	bed
birth	being born
coarse	not fine
course	path, series
device	(noun)
devise	(verb)
forth	forward
fourth	4th
peace	not war
piece	a portion

2. Spelling Rules

Unfortunately, almost all spelling rules have exceptions. Nevertheless, some of the rules may help you to spell common words that give you trouble, especially those words formed with suffixes.

a. Final silent *e*

Drop a final silent *e* before suffixes beginning with a vowel (*-ing*, *-age*, *-able*).

hope + ing = hoping
plume + age = plumage
love + able = lovable

Keep a final silent *e* before suffixes beginning with a consonant (*-ful, -ly, -ness*).

hope + ful = hopeful
sincere + ly = sincerely
pale + ness = paleness

Note the following exceptions.

| dyeing | hoeing | judgment | awful |
| ninth | truly | duly | wholly |

The *e* is retained in such words as the following in order to keep the soft sound of the *c* and *g*.

| noticeable | courageous |
| peaceable | outrageous |

b. Doubling final consonant

When you add a suffix beginning with a vowel to words ending in one consonant preceded by one vowel (*red, redder*), notice where the word is accented. If it is accented on the last syllable or if it is a monosyllable, double the final consonant.

prefer + ed = preferred   benefit + ed = benefited
omit + ing = omitting   profit + ing = profiting

Note that in some words the accent shifts when the suffix is added.

| referred | reference |
| prefer | preference |

There are some exceptions to this rule.

transferable   excellent

Many words that should follow this rule have alternative spellings.

worshiped/worshipped
traveling/travelling

c. Words ending in *y*

If the *y* is preceded by a consonant, change the *y* to *i* before any suffix except *-ing*.

lady + es = ladies   carry + ing = carrying
try + ed = tried   study + ing = studying

The *y* is usually retained if it is preceded by a vowel.

valleys   monkeys   displayed

Note the following exceptions.

laid   paid   said   ladylike

d. *ie* or *ei*

When *ie* or *ei* is used to spell the sound *ee*, remember the old rule "*i* before *e*, except after *c*."

achieve   ceiling
belief   conceit
field   receive

Note the following exceptions.

either   leisure   neither   seize   weird

3. Hyphenation

A hyphen is used, under certain circumstances, to join the parts of compound words. When in doubt, consult your dictionary.

a. Compound adjectives

Hyphenate words used as a single adjective before a noun.

far-reaching proposal   old-fashioned attitude
well-informed leader   matter-of-fact statement

When these compound adjectives follow the noun, they are usually not hyphenated.

The snow-covered mountains lay ahead.

The mountains ahead were snow covered.

When an adverb ending in -*ly* is used with an adjective or a participle, do not hyphenate the compound.

highly praised organization

widely advertised product

b. Prefixes

When a prefix retains its original strength in the compound, use a hyphen. In most instances, however, the prefix has been absorbed into the word and should not be separated by a hyphen.

> ex-president, excommunicate

> pre-Christian, preconception

In some words a hyphen indicates a difference in meaning.

> She recovered her strength.

> She re-covered her sofa.

c. Numbers

Use a hyphen when writing out the numbers twenty-one through ninety-nine.

> twenty-six

> one hundred sixty-three

Hyphenate the numerator and denominator of a fraction.

> two-thirds

d. Suspensive hyphen

When two compound words are connected by *and* or *or* and the second word in both compounds is the same, you may indicate the first compound by writing just its first word followed by a hyphen and a space.

> full- or part-time employment

Chapter 21

Exercise 1 Final Silent e

Write the correct spelling of each word indicated below.

1. argue + ing
2. imagine + able
3. gentle + ness
4. notice + ing
5. purpose + ly
6. time + ing
7. awe + ful
8. trace + able
9. judge + ing
10. time + ly
11. glare + ing
12. peace + ful

Chapter *21*

Exercise 2 Doubling Final Consonant

Write the correct spelling of each word. Be prepared to give the reasons for your answers.

1. avid + ly
2. repel + ent
3. even + ness
4. snob + ish
5. label + ed
6. fret + ful
7. offer + ed
8. scan + ing
9. armor + ed
10. entrap + ment
11. remit + ance
12. tip + ed

Chapter 21

Exercise 3 Words Ending in y

Write the correct spelling of each word.

1. easy + ness
2. play + ful
3. cry + ed
4. baby + es
5. moody + er
6. annoy + ed
7. fry + ing
8. lovely + er
9. terrify + ed
10. lobby + ing

Chapter 21

Exercise 4 Hyphenation

Decide whether the compounds in the following sentences should be written solid, with a hyphen, or as two words. Correct them, consulting a dictionary if necessary.

1. Your far fetched idea is extremely badly conceived.
2. A partially filled freezer wastes more energy than one that is completely full does.
3. Half time employees must attend the seminar for a half hour.
4. This is a badly designed building.
5. That is a well designed building.
6. The two toned car is now rust covered.
7. A gray haired woman offered me assistance in crossing the one way street.
8. The fund raisers insisted that the money they had raised so far was only a drop in the bucket.
9. The strong willed child drew more attention than the step mother wanted.
10. He is a true believer.

Chapter 21

Exercise 5 Words Commonly Misspelled

In the spaces, fill in the letter or letters needed to complete each word. If no letter is needed, leave the space empty.

1. suc _____ es _____ ful
2. equip _____ ed
3. prof _____ es _____ or
4. tra _____ gedy
5. marr _____ ge
6. dis _____ ap _____ ear _____ ed
7. argu _____ ment
8. relig _____ s
9. com _____ it _____ ment
10. becom _____ ing
11. ar _____ tic
12. hum _____ rous
13. har _____ as _____
14. practic _____ ly
15. depend _____ ncy
16. ap _____ ar _____ nt
17. def _____ n _____ tely
18. trul _____ y
19. un _____ atural

Chapter 21

Exercise 6 *Similar Words Frequently Confused*

Underline the correct word in each pair.

1. When (your/you're) fighting for a (principal/principle), (it's/its) crucial to gather a strong (corps/corpse) of supporters.
2. Once you have found the (personal/personnel) you require, you all need to decide what (affect/effect) you wish to accomplish.
3. (Counsel/Council) from similar groups may be more useful (than/then) you expect.
4. There will never be complete (ascent/assent) on any issue, but each individual's point of view will help (complement/compliment) everyone else's position.
5. For the (dual/duel) purposes of raising money and raising the public's (conscience/consciousness), your group will need to (device/devise) a plan, even if you must (altar/alter) it later.
6. (Its/It's) purpose is to keep everyone from (loosing/losing) heart and thinking success is only an (allusion/illusion).

Chapter 21

Exercise 7 Similar Words Frequently Confused

Underline the correct word in each pair.

1. Preparing for a vacation before you leave is (quiet/quite) important, (weather/whether) you will be away for a week or a month.
2. Obviously, you need to consider where (your/you're) going—to a (desert/dessert) (aisle/isle), to a large metropolis, or just across the state (boarder/border).
3. (Your/You're) destination will (affect/effect) many decisions, such as what (cloths/clothes) you need to pack.
4. (Access/Excess) luggage can be a real burden, unless you plan to remain (stationary/stationery) during the entire trip.
5. You also need to (choose/chose) how (formally/formerly) you want to map out (your/you're) itinerary.
6. (Their/There/They're) are (to/too/two) many people who plan (their/there/they're) vacations down to the very minute and (than/then) (their/there/they're) (to/too/two) tired (to/too/two) enjoy themselves.
7. Take some (advice/advise): plan now, but make sure you have time to relax (later/latter).

22 *Mechanics*

The appearance of your paper, like the appearance of a person, reflects your attitude toward yourself, the subject, and your audience. Mechanics—capital letters, numbers, abbreviations, and italics—may seem unimportant compared with some of the larger concerns of writing. However, accurate use of mechanics suggests your confidence and authority, and it will help you gain the respect and attention of your readers.

1. Capital Letters

a. Capitalizing proper nouns

Usually, proper nouns are capitalized and common nouns not. A common noun is a general term: *author, city, building*. A proper noun is the name of a particular person, place, or thing: *Edith Wharton, San Francisco, the Capitol*. Other proper nouns that need to be capitalized include the following:

Days of the week, months, and holidays: *Labor Day*
Most organizations: *Department of the Interior*
Members of organizations: *Girl Scouts*
Historic events, periods, and documents: *Middle Ages*
Specific places and geographical areas: *the Midwest*
Names of races, ethnic groups, and languages: *African-American*
Names of religions, religious figures and holidays, and sacred books:
    Day of Atonement
Registered trademarks: *Alpo*
Terms identifying family members only when used in place of proper
    names: *My sister received a letter from Grandmother.*
Titles of persons when they precede proper names: *Mayor Dinkins*
When used without proper names, only titles of high rank: *Both Mayor
    Mason and the postmaster of our town appealed to the Postmaster General.*
Names of genera but not of species: *Homo sapiens*
Stars, constellations, and planets, but not the earth, sun, or moon un-
    less used as astronomical names: *Jupiter*

b. Capitalizing titles

The first word and the important words of the titles of books, plays, musical compositions, pictures, and other artistic works: *Bruce Springsteen's "Born in the USA."*

c. Capitalizing sentences and quotations

Capitalize the first word of every sentence. Capitalize the first word of every direct quotation:

"Come to see me in my office," said Professor McFadden. "I will be happy to read your rough drafts."

Following a colon, capitalize the first words in a series of short questions:

The first-aid questions were important: What are the first signs of shock in an accident victim? Should she be kept warm? Should she eat? Should she drink?

Capitalize the first word of every line of poetry unless the poem itself does not use a capital letter.

2. Numbers

Be consistent: do not use words for some numbers and figures for others.

Usually write out numbers from one to ten and round numbers that can be expressed in one or two words: *seven hundred people.*

Write out adjectival forms of numbers when they can be expressed in one or two words: *the ten-thousandth customer.*

To indicate a range of numbers, use the complete second number up to 99: *44–48, 92–99.*

For larger numbers, use the last two digits of the second number, unless more are required: *125–28* and *12,500–13,000.*

Use figures to express the day of the month and the year in a date: *September 16, 1960* and *15 July 1958.*

Usually write out centuries and decades, but you may express them in figures. In the latter case, the figures are followed by an *s* without an apostrophe: *the sixties, the 1960s, the '60s.*

Use figures for numbers in street addresses, long numbers, chapter and page numbers, time citations followed directly by *A.M.* or *P.M.*, and decimals: *page 33, 8.5 percent, 9:00 P.M.*

Use figures with abbreviations and symbols: *55 mph, 80 lbs.*

Use figures after a dollar sign: *$12.50.* If the amount of money can be expressed in one or two words, you may write it out: *sixteen dollars.*

3. Abbreviations

Use abbreviations very sparingly in expository prose. As a general rule, spell out the first names of people, the words in addresses, the days of the week and the months of the year, and units of measurement:

> Elliot Brodie of 327 West Oakland Avenue, Kenosha, Wisconsin, moved on December 16, 1989.

Some abbreviations are always written with periods: *Ph.D., i.e., etc.* Others are written without periods: *TX, CA, IRS.* Acronyms are written without periods: *UNICEF, NATO.* Some abbreviations may be written with or without periods, so consult a dictionary: *USA* or *U.S.A.*

Usually write out civil, religious, military, and academic titles: *Senator Kennedy, Colonel Jackson.* Such titles may be abbreviated only when followed by the person's full name: *Sen. Edward Kennedy.*

Abbreviate certain titles when they precede names: *Ms., Dr.*

After names, abbreviate titles and degrees: *Julia Hart, Ph.D.*

Do not duplicate a title before and after a name. This is incorrect: *Dr. Julia Hart, Ph.D.*

Write out the words *volume, chapter, edition,* and *page* in references within a text; abbreviate them in parenthetical citations and bibliographies:

> I found the quotation on page 267 of the third edition.

In technical writing, abbreviate terms of measurement when used with figures: *4 hrs., 12 ft.*

Use the ampersand (&) and abbreviations such as *Co., Inc.,* and *Bros.* only when a company uses such an abbreviation in its official title.

Abbreviations that end in a period form their plurals by adding *'s: two M.D.'s.*

Abbreviations that do not end in a period usually form their plurals by adding *s: the PTAs of both schools.*

4. Italics

In the titles of books, monographs, musical works, and such separate publications, italicize all words: *The Blithedale Romance, Pride and Preju-*

dice. In the titles of newspapers and periodicals, italicize only the distinctive words:

the *New York Times,* the *Southern Review*

Italicize foreign words that have not yet become accepted in the English language:

The dancer unties a knot with her feet in the Mexican *reboza.*

Italicize the scientific names for plants and animals: *Cyanocitta stellera.* Italicize the names of ships, trains, and planes, but not the names of the companies that own them:

United's *Royal Hawaiian* flight

Italicize words, letters, or figures used as such:

The misuse of *cool* and *real* is a common fault.

Chapter 22

Exercise 1 Mechanics

Underline and correct any errors in capitalization, numbers, abbreviations, and italics.

1. In the middle of Ca.'s San Francisco bay lies an isolated rock that is a famous Island: Alcatraz.

2. Some people may know about the place from the movie the Birdman Of Alcatraz.

3. In the early Nineteenth Century, the 12½-acre island was used as a fort, the final barricade between S.F. and its enemies.

4. Around the time of the civil war, the fortress became a Military prison, and the giant guns were moved to the base of the Golden Gate bridge several mi. away.

5. Military prisoners were considered the worst of criminals because they had dishonored their country as well as broken its Laws, so Alcatraz prison was built with few, if any, amenities.

6. Cells were dank, three-ft.-by-eight-ft. rooms bordered on 3 sides by stone and on the 4th by a solid windowless door, so that some prisoners rarely saw the Sun.

7. When the Warden locked the prisoners in their cells at night, he confined them to dark, airless holes; the cells lacked electricity, ventilation, & plumbing.

8. In the 1930's, growing crime rates and the development of Organized Crime persuaded Federal authorities that Alcatraz should be expanded into a nonmilitary Prison for incorrigible and dangerous inmates.

9. Alcatraz's natural surroundings made it very secure because the freezing temp. and the strong current of San Francisco bay made swimming to shore unlikely, and the no. of guards per inmate made hijacking a boat impossible.

10. 265–275 inmates were housed in Alcatraz during its heyday, with a ratio of 1 Guard to every 2 prisoners.

11. Eleven times per day, at the same time every day, Guards would line the inmates up for "counts," during which all the prisoners would be counted to ensure none had escaped; the Warden would call for surprise cts. as frequently as 2× per hr. to catch prisoners unaware.

12. Prison conditions were desolate: inmates—with only 2 blankets & a pillow—slept on 2-legged cots that hooked on the walls of the cells, and although cell doors were replaced with bars, Guards had felt pads on their shoes to allow them to move around the Prison noiselessly.

13. In spite of the poor conditions, Alcatraz had some advantages; prisoners had their cells to themselves, and they were allowed to order books and certain magazines, such as The Atlantic monthly, from the Prison Library.

14. In Nineteen Sixty-three, the Government closed Alcatraz because of the cost of keeping prisoners segregated and because of the American Public's outcry about cruel conditions there.

Chapter 22

Exercise 2 Mechanics

Underline and correct any errors in capitalization, numbers, abbreviations, and italics.

1. Although an experimental Television Station went on the air in nineteen twenty-eight, broadcasting did not become regular until April thirtieth, 1929, when president Roosevelt opened the New York world's fair.
2. Surprisingly, the 1st color broadcast took place that same year.
3. Early shows were usually produced by sponsors, such as *General electric,* that had total control not just of advertising but also of the content of the programs; after a while, Networks began to produce their own shows and sold only spots for ads. to sponsors.
4. Most broadcasting stopped during world war Two, but soon after that it flourished, and some shows were introduced that would still be familiar decades later, like "I love Lucy."
5. Of course, many other shows from that 1950–1 season, such as "Men against crime" and "Hands of destiny," are forgotten in the Nineteen Nineties.
6. A # of the longest-running shows in history came into existence in the 40's and 50's; one of the most memorable is "The Ed Sullivan show" (1948–71), which people tuned into every Sun. eve.
7. "Dragnet" (1955–1975) introduced a character people remember today: sergeant Joe Friday.
8. Despite the popularity of some old shows and plot lines, viewing tastes require that programming be changed from yr. to yr., in part so that it will reflect current events and concerns; for example, whereas in 1956 only 2 crime series were on the air, 20 yrs. later the total was 18.
9. The situation comedy has remained a popular format, with 100s produced over the years.
10. Some critics speculate that the Viewer actually enjoys the predictability of such programs (much as some readers enjoy the repeated plots in Romance novels).
11. A demanding market means that the President and Management of a station such as CBS or N.B.C. give a new show less than a full season to prove its worth.
12. Budgets are certainly a factor, since the cost of producing a ½-hr. show doubled between 1970 and 1980.
13. Viewers may be assured, if not reassured, that while subject matter may change, t.v. will probably be in 10 years very much what it is today.